Advance Praise for
Unshackled

"If we are to guarantee every child in America the right to rise, we must be willing to reimagine and rethink our education-delivery system. With this book, Bolick and Hardiman offer a path forward to a transformed system that would unlock opportunity and lifelong success for each and every child."

—Governor Jeb Bush, chair, Foundation for Excellence in Education

"What would the K–12 school system look like if you started from scratch? Bolick and Hardiman point out that education wouldn't be shackled by a bureaucratic and inefficient government monopoly on the service. The authors make a convincing and data-driven case to fund students directly instead of school systems."

—Corey DeAngelis, director of school choice, Reason Foundation

"A jedi and a padawan of the school choice universe wrote a book. America's kids will be better for it. I've known Clint for almost twenty years and Kate for about two. Clint has changed the world a lot and I expect the same from Kate. This book is, I hope, just the first step in a long-standing and profound collaboration."

—Derrell Bradford, executive vice president, 50CAN

UNSHACKLED

UNSHACKLED

FREEING AMERICA'S K–12 EDUCATION SYSTEM

Clint Bolick and Kate J. Hardiman

HOOVER INSTITUTION PRESS
STANFORD UNIVERSITY   STANFORD, CALIFORNIA

hoover.org

Hoover Institution Press Publication No. 718

Hoover Institution at Leland Stanford Junior University,
Stanford, California 94305-6003

First printing 2020
27 26 25 24 23 22 21 20   9 8 7 6 5 4 3 2 1

Manufactured in the United States of America
Printed on acid-free archival-quality paper

Library of Congress Control Number: 2020944236

ISBN 978-0-8179-2445-4 (pbk)
ISBN 978-0-8179-2446-1 (epub)
ISBN 978-0-8179-2447-8 (mobi)
ISBN 978-0-8179-2448-5 (PDF)

For my granddaughter Madelyn, and her future. —CB

To my former students, for their daily display of faith and perseverance. May we create a better education system for your children. —KJH

Contents

Preface

Clint Bolick

Why is a judge coauthoring a book about education reform?

My work on this book was not part of my day job, of course, but rather through my affiliation as a research fellow with the Hoover Institution, which provides a valuable outlet for writing and speaking on important issues. Most of those efforts are focused on law, but this book is not.

Like many lawyers—I would venture to guess, an ever-increasing number —I started out teaching. From my earliest memories, I always wanted to be a teacher. And in college, I set out to do exactly that. As a student at Drew University in New Jersey, I enrolled in a reciprocal teacher-training program at the nearby College of St. Elizabeth, a women's Catholic college, where for most of my time I was the only male student. It was the first time I had ever set foot in a Catholic institution of any kind.

Through that program, I interned and student-taught at the high school and middle school levels. My internship in an inner-city high school was transformative. Growing up in a Newark suburb, my own public school academic experience was far from exemplary, but I gained the skills necessary to become the first person in my family to graduate from college.

But most of the low-income students who attended the school in which I interned would never have such opportunities. In fact, given the disorder that surrounded them, they were lucky if they survived the experience, much less graduated from high school and went on to college or productive livelihoods. That experience, I learned, was more the norm than the exception for economically disadvantaged youngsters who desperately need high-quality educational opportunities to succeed.

At the same time as I was interning and student teaching, I took a course at Drew in constitutional law. That, too, was transformative. Most inspiring, unsurprisingly, was *Brown v. Board of Education.* In that case, a passionate and determined lawyer named Thurgood Marshall and his talented and creative colleagues demanded an end to separate and unequal educational opportunities. And the United States Supreme Court proclaimed that, henceforth, educational opportunities would be provided to all students on equal terms.

My tandem experiences as a student teacher and in constitutional law provided me with two insights. First, that although decades had passed since *Brown*, America's education system was still largely separate and unequal, startlingly deficient in providing high-quality opportunities to children who most need them. Second, following Thurgood Marshall's inspiration, that I could accomplish more to expand those opportunities in the courtroom than in the classroom.

Fortunately, I had the tremendous opportunity to work as a public interest litigator and to help defend the nation's first inner-city school voucher program in Milwaukee in the early 1990s. Other legal battles followed, including defending a scholarship tax credit in the court in which I am honored to now serve (I certainly never imagined that when I first argued there!). Those battles culminated in the landmark 2003 Supreme Court decision *Zelman v. Simmons-Harris*, which upheld the constitutionality of the Cleveland school voucher program. I recounted those twelve years of litigation in an earlier book, *Voucher Wars: Waging the Legal Battle over School Choice.*

One of those experiences echoes in recent events. On April 29, 1992, a colleague and I were in South-Central Los Angeles to meet with low-income parents who wanted to secure a better education for their children. Unfortunately, it was the same day as the acquittal of police officers who had beaten Rodney King. My colleague and I were among the first people attacked as riots broke out while we were driving to the meeting. Not fully apprehending the danger, and because parents had braved the disturbance to meet with us, we proceeded with the meeting. Afterward, we barely escaped with our lives as we navigated the violence to return safely to our downtown hotel. But the families could not leave, and despite our efforts in court, their children remained trapped in failing schools. That widespread protests against injustice have emerged again nearly thirty years later demonstrates how little of the needed systemic change we have accomplished.

During my litigation career, I was often opposite people of good faith who were equally committed to high-quality education but who believed that private school choice would harm public education. Although I strongly disagree and believe that the record abundantly demonstrates otherwise, I have always wanted to expand my focus to more fully encompass public school reform. After all, the vast majority of American children attend public schools, and indeed my own four kids have never spent a day in a private school. I was privileged to serve on three boards of innovative public charter schools: Basis Schools, Great Hearts Academies, and schools sponsored by the Challenge Foundation. But I have always wanted to join hands with those who desire to bring about reform and improvement in traditional public schools.

Over my decades as a lawyer, I have spoken on education issues at dozens of law schools across the country. Always there were one or more students whose paths to law school were similar to mine. Many of them are former public school teachers, often through programs like Teach for America. Although most of them came from affluent backgrounds, their teaching experiences in dangerous or appallingly low-performing schools opened their eyes and motivated them to seek change, some of them as lawyers. Whether they are liberal or conservative or somewhere in between, I feel great kinship with these reformers.

One of those talented young reformers is my coauthor, Kate Hardiman. When I first met Kate, she was a student at the University of Notre Dame and set on a career first as a teacher, then as a lawyer. She had also taken an influential class in education law and policy and wrote her senior thesis on the legality and morality of school choice programs, using the Indiana voucher program as a case study.

After graduation, Kate became a teaching fellow with the Alliance for Catholic Education and taught English in a Catholic inner-city high school in Chicago. In that position, Kate was able to experience the tremendous benefits of private, faith-based education for economically disadvantaged inner-city schoolchildren. While teaching, she also began writing in earnest on education policy issues for the *Washington Examiner* and other outlets. Now an evening student at Georgetown Law Center, Kate also works as a full-time legal fellow at Cooper & Kirk PLLC, a constitutional litigation firm in

Washington, DC. Kate plans to devote her legal career to education reform. We need many more committed, talented, and energetic reformers like her.

In our conversations, Kate and I came to realize that no one had yet written a book presenting a comprehensive vision of education reform: not top-down, one-size-fits-all education but an environment where the talents of educators and principals can be unleashed to produce high-quality educational environments in the midst of abundant options. We decided to write that book, and in these pages we humbly present our vision. Although this is fully a collaborative effort, throughout the book we have interspersed personal comments reflecting our individual experiences.

Although I am now removed from direct involvement in public policy, my years as a judge have only strengthened my passion for education reform. Nearly every serious criminal case that comes before us involves young men who never had a chance. As a society we have finite influence over the lot into which children are born, but we do have great influence over whether and how they are educated. Both Kate and I, as well as many of you reading this book, have witnessed the soaring prospects that high-quality education can deliver, as well as the stultifying futures to which poor education too often consigns vulnerable children.

Judges rarely write books on public policy, owing perhaps to few of them coming from public-policy backgrounds. Some do, perhaps most notably Richard Posner on the US Court of Appeals for the Seventh Circuit, who has written on myriad topics ranging from capitalism to national emergencies to the Clinton impeachment. Justice William O. Douglas published books on environmental policy, Latin American politics, and global federalism. Recently, many state supreme court justices have spoken out on reforms they support in the criminal justice system. Though judges may comment on policy, we must be careful not to commit ourselves to positions on specific legal issues and must recuse ourselves from cases in which our impartiality might reasonably be questioned.

But we—judges, lawyers, and teachers alike—remain citizens, and all Americans are deeply impacted by our education system. All of us, regardless of our perspectives, have an important role to play in expanding educational opportunities. Our nation is deeply and bitterly divided over so many issues, not least education policy. Our nation's children cannot afford for us to remain polarized.

In *Unshackled*, Kate Hardiman and I offer a hopeful vision of a transformed education system that empowers families, teachers, and others who have a stake in successful outcomes to have a much greater impact in providing high-quality educational opportunities. We fervently hope that everyone who reads this book will find some ideas worth considering, and that some will find many of them meritorious. Most of all, we hope the ideas we present will spark earnest conversation about systemic reform based on a central provocative question: What type of education system would we create if we were starting afresh today?

CHAPTER 1

Reimagining American Public Education

Take a moment for a thought experiment.

If you were creating the ideal American elementary and secondary education system from scratch, with absolutely no preconceptions derived from the current system and with the full range of technological tools at your disposal, what would it look like?

If you give this exercise even a modicum of thought, chances are that the model you come up with would look little like the ossified, monopolistic, monolithic, top-down, bureaucratic, command-and-control, hidebound, wasteful, inefficient, brick-and-mortar, one-size-fits-all, special-interest-dominated system to which most of America's children are consigned.

Education is America's great conundrum. Its structure and outcomes have largely remained the same since the early 1900s despite waves of "reform" and a rapidly evolving society. We are the greatest, freest, most productive nation in the world, yet our primary and secondary educational system is mediocre compared to those of other industrialized nations. Though there is seemingly little that anyone agrees on in American public life these days, the general consensus is (and has been for decades) that something is wrong with our public education system.

The best and brightest students from the entire globe flock to our nation's colleges and universities, yet our K–12 schools are so feeble that most high school graduates need remedial courses when they get to college. We remain the most cutting-edge nation in terms of technological innovation, yet our educational institutions are largely untouched, and certainly untransformed, by the breathtaking advances that have profoundly affected and improved almost every other aspect of our lives. We spend more on K–12 education than almost every other nation, yet our fiercest international competitors produce far-better-educated students for less money. Our educational system produces only a fraction of the skilled workers needed for high-tech jobs. We cannot continue to compete effectively in a global economy if our educational system continues to produce such dismal results.

Our education system not only fails to reflect our national commitments; it rejects them.

We measure educational quality in terms of dollars spent rather than results obtained, with little accountability for the allocation of billions in taxpayer funds.

We believe in merit-based compensation, yet we pay teachers based largely on seniority, not for how much students learn.

We are averse to bureaucracies, yet we spend lavishly on administrators who contribute little to the educational enterprise, and they are paid far higher salaries than our best teachers.

We have well-intentioned philanthropic funders from the technology sector who invest in the stagnant status quo rather than in bringing disruptive innovation to the educational marketplace in ways that fueled their own entrepreneurial success.

We made a solemn commitment more than sixty years ago to provide equal educational opportunities for all American children regardless of race; yet despite enormous investments, the vast majority of students trapped in failing public schools are those who need education improvements the most, including low-income and minority schoolchildren.

We embrace choice and competition for virtually every important product and service in our lives, but we resist choice and competition for the service most central to our children's future.

If someone who lived in the late 1800s were to teleport to the present day, that person would recognize almost nothing about life in America. Nothing, that is, except our schools, which have changed remarkably little in the last 125 years. Most students still attend the brick-and-mortar school assigned based on their zip code (though these schools are now far larger). They sit in rows focused (or not) on one teacher in the front of the classroom. The schools are organized into districts whose boundaries are usually unchanged, despite shifting demographics. That nineteenth-century factory model adequately served generations of American students (less so those who were segregated into inferior schools) through much of the twentieth century. Yet it works poorly for most children in the twenty-first century. Sadly, we are bound to that system by nostalgia, inertia, lack of imagination, and the political muscle of some of the nation's most powerful special-interest groups.

Were we to loosen those bonds, we would enable our largely untapped capacity to deliver a personalized, high-quality education to every student. Education that reflects the values, abilities, needs, interests, and aspirations of children and their families. Education that harnesses our technological power and can be accessed in traditional settings, at home, or in a blended experience. Education that equips American students for the ever-evolving challenges that will determine our nation's future freedom and prosperity on the world stage.

This book is primarily about the policy changes necessary to bring our educational system, perhaps kicking and screaming, into the twenty-first century. Although we highlight many effective educational models and innovations in the following chapters, we do not prescribe all of them for all students. We have had far too many prescriptions from self-styled experts who "know what works," and we have wasted precious resources in pursuit of educational conformity. Instead, we propose policies to facilitate innovation, reward excellence, increase parental choice, and promote accountability. With enough options and the power to choose among them, families can determine what works best for their children, those who contribute most to the educational process will be rewarded, and success can be replicated.

Creating a twenty-first-century educational system requires a willingness to embrace fundamental change, which in turn calls upon us to diagnose the current system's failures and learn from several decades of failed or low-impact reforms. As we develop further in subsequent chapters, a clear-eyed assessment of the status quo yields at least ten basic principles, all of them interrelated and mutually reinforcing, that should guide a transformative education policy agenda. We should measure *every* education policy by these principles:

The school system is a means to an end, not an end in itself.

We are mired in educational mediocrity and dysfunction in large part because we confuse means and ends. Schools were created because they were an efficient and effective way to educate students. Often, they still are. But if they ever cease to be the optimal way to educate children, or if they are not the best means of educating a particular child, the system should not be exalted to the detriment of each child's learning and development.

The most frequent and effective accusation hurled against any type of meaningful education reform is that it will hurt public schools. In nearly all instances, those challenges arise when a proposal permits public funds to flow to schools other than traditional public schools, which is conflated with hurting public schools. If traditional public schools provided an optimal education to every child, then as a matter of public policy, we should support them exclusively. But they don't, which means we face a choice between supporting schools as ends in themselves, regardless of how well or poorly they perform, or enabling students to pursue educational opportunities in some other fashion. Those who genuinely care about our children's future should focus less on defending systems, whatever they are, and instead dedicate themselves to enabling students to achieve their full potential.

Public education should be concerned about whether, not where, kids are learning.

Related to the first principle is the crucial conceptual difference between public *schools* and public *education*. Education can take place in a public school, some other type of school, at home, in front of a computer screen, or in some hybrid experience. When a student sits in a public school learning little, the obligation (guaranteed in every state's constitution) of providing a public education is not advanced. Children learning in a private school or at home advance the goals of public education, even though they are not in a public school.

Much of the energy against education reform is directed toward preventing children from pursuing options outside traditional public schools, even where many of those schools are failing and alternatives exist. When such efforts deprive children of high-quality educational opportunities, they do not advance the goals of public education; they defeat them.

Education policy should be about kids, not adults.

Too often debates over education policy are driven by what benefits the grown-ups in the system rather than what tangibly benefits children. That gets the public education equation exactly backward: decisions should be made based on what benefits students.

No one in our society provides a more important service than the men and women educating our children. Those who do so effectively should be rewarded commensurately (later on, we explore ways to do that far more generously and effectively than we do today). But public schools are not a jobs program. We need to attract the best and the brightest to the vital task of education while refusing to subsidize mediocrity and unnecessary bureaucracy. Every education policy should be assessed on how and whether it will benefit students.

We should recognize that every child is different.

All children have unique needs, talents, aspirations, and personalities, yet most schools are not organized to effectively teach children as individuals. For the past century and a half, K–12 education has been about grouping children: into grades based on their age; into schools according to their zip code; into school districts according to arbitrary and obsolete (and sometimes impenetrable) boundaries; into classes according to their perceived abilities. Teachers often teach to the middle, leaving brighter students bored and more challenged students behind.

Traditional public schools are remarkably inflexible. Try getting an advanced middle school student into high school classes—a nearly impossible feat in most districts. Try getting extra help or resources for a student who has difficulty with certain tasks without going through the painstaking process of having your child declared learning-disabled (even if the student does not have a disability) and obtaining an individualized education plan. Imagine how difficult it is for parents who themselves lack education or resources to obtain individualized services for their children, especially in a massive, impersonal school district.

Technology makes "groupified" learning obsolete. Integrating computers as an important part of the learning environment allows students to proceed at their own pace in every subject. One child may have a talent or passion for math, another for language or science or writing. Frequent testing indicates when students have achieved mastery or need extra help. Customized instruction is highly flexible and efficient, providing education tailored to each child's unique needs and abilities.

Schools should operate like businesses.

Another effective reform opposition tactic is to decry proposed changes as "privatization" that would turn public schools into the likes of McDonald's. We should ask ourselves why those arguments are persuasive. We rely on private businesses to provide the vast majority of goods and services. They generally do a good job, and those that don't go out of business. And at Burger King, you can "have it your way," whereas at most public schools (or other government service providers), you emphatically cannot.

Many of our reform proposals involve injecting greater choice, competition, and business principles into the education enterprise. We recognize that at least for the foreseeable future, most education will be provided by government actors. But the rules of economics are not suspended at the schoolhouse doors: public schools can and do respond to market forces like consumer choice. Whether as taxpayers, parents, or even teachers employed in public schools, we should welcome and not fear this development. For those who champion educational opportunities for children, the fact that they may be provided by someone outside of the public sector does not discount the possibility that they may provide excellent services. And importantly, such providers face consequences for failure.

Power over education should be allocated to those who have the greatest stake in children's success.

Many debates over education policy focus on money, specifically how much is spent and whether it is equally distributed. To stoke systemic change, we need to worry less about money and focus more on *power* (including who controls the vast amounts of money spent on public education). In our public schools today, politicians have power. School boards have power. Bureaucrats have power. Unions have power. Principals, who are answerable to superintendents, who are answerable to politicians, who are answerable to those who supported their campaigns, do not have power commensurate with the central role they play in the effective delivery of educational services. Teachers, at least individually, do not have power, even though they affect educational outcomes much more than anyone else. Most unfortunately, many parents, especially those who are poor, do not have power, despite the fact that they have the greatest stake in their children's opportunities and success.

We need to reverse that perverse misallocation of power. Those with the greatest stake in and responsibility for children's educational success lack the essential power to control outcomes. They are subject to the whims, caprice, self-interest, and misguided best intentions of those who are not directly responsible for children's success. Schools themselves should have authority to direct resources as their needs dictate, as well as control over personnel decisions. Public policy should be measured by how much power it provides to those on the educational front lines: principals, teachers, and especially parents.

Funds should be allocated toward students, not schools.

The most effective way to transfer power over education is through the purse strings. Private businesses must attract and satisfy customers to survive. Most governmental entities do not. Funding for government entities is a *political* decision, meaning that those who desire increased funding apply pressure to elected officials rather than appealing to consumers. This is not entirely true for public schools—many are funded partly on a per-capita basis, that is, based on the number of students—but funding is primarily a decision made by state legislators or school district officials.

Imagine the transformation if students were the primary source of public school funding. Schools would be focused on attracting and retaining students by offering a distinctive, high-quality, responsive educational product. The power of politicians and special-interest groups would be reduced. The biggest beneficiaries would be low- to middle-income parents, who lack any real power in the current system. Placing at their disposal the significant resources expended on their education would shift power with great consequence. "Backpack funding," where the money follows the children to their school of choice, must be a central feature of systemic education reform.

Variety should be the spice of education.

Public schools are, by and large, remarkably homogenous. Chances are that on any given day, most schools in a district—or an entire state—will be teaching the same thing at the same time in the same way. Common Core (though many states have rejected it and some never implemented it) arguably exacerbated this standardization.

Educational options should be as numerous and varied as the students who pursue them. Families should be able to choose from a menu of alternatives, even combining public and nonpublic education. Schools should be free to break the mold to serve their students and control their own budgets, unleashing their untapped potential. We should encourage innovation both inside and outside the public schools and allow students to mix and match options that best match their needs and abilities.

Education providers should be held responsible for outcomes.

For the freest nation on earth, our K–12 school system is amazingly prescriptive. The government tells public schools what they must teach, when they must teach it, who they can hire, what salaries they must pay, and so on. Public education focuses on inputs, not outcomes. Who cares if teachers who can't teach are certified? Who cares if the best teachers have never spent a day in education school?

We should worry less about how schools operate and more about whether they are effective. That doesn't necessarily translate into a standardized testing regime, but it does require us to effectively measure progress and achievement. Vast strides have been made in measuring value added—that is, how much a student progresses in light of where that student started. We should generously reward schools and teachers that take underperforming students and move them to grade level. Bad teachers should be fired and bad schools closed; good teachers should be well compensated, and effective educational providers rewarded.

Reforms should be adopted with an urgency that reflects the reality.

How many times have we embraced broad, sweeping national or state-level reforms that promise results over the long term? They have rarely fulfilled their great promise, despite consuming large sums of taxpayer and philanthropic dollars. Worst of all, they provide false promise to families and students who need results not at some point in the future but *today*. Our policy agenda should reflect the short time horizon that students have: a child who cannot read after third grade may never remediate; a student who lacks basic skills in high school has little hope of graduation, college, or a productive livelihood.

If we cannot produce a school system that provides a high-quality education to the vast majority of students, we should at least have an exit strategy for families to pursue different options. Whatever we do, we must realize that the one commodity in the shortest supply is *time*.

Distilled to their essence, these principles might be referred to as two Cs and two Ds. These are not grades one wants to receive in school, but they are the drivers of systemic education reform: choice, competition, deregulation, and decentralization.

Choice and competition are the external drivers of educational improvement for public schools. They also expand the opportunity for more individualized educational opportunities, as well as create an escape valve for students trapped by their zip code in failing public schools.

But choice and competition are not panaceas. Most children will continue to rely on public schools. Those schools must be able to effectively respond to their students' needs and harness tools to effectively deliver high-quality education. To accomplish this, we must devolve power and accountability to the school level.

As we write, our nation as a whole is experiencing a profoundly transformative experience in responding to the COVID-19 coronavirus. In particular, our schools and children have faced educational upheaval like never before. Nearly every school closed. Schools have been forced to deliver educational services online; some have succeeded heroically, while others were completely unprepared to make this shift. As a result, Americans have witnessed great disparities in the educational services schools are able to provide amid changed circumstances. And while many are stepping up to these extreme challenges, too often the system is failing to come close to providing the educational experiences they are supposed to deliver.

Those challenges have forced all of us to reconsider the status quo. We hope that the response to the COVID-19 crisis will have helped empower parents rather than discourage them. Some may be empowered to continue at-home education for their children. Others may be empowered by learning whether or not their school was prepared to transition to a different mode of learning. Still others may appreciate what technology has to offer in helping their children learn. And all of us have gained even greater appreciation for those especially remarkable teachers behind the scenes who make education happen in the midst of a national crisis.

Although we began researching and writing this book before the pandemic struck, the experience reinforced the principles for effectively delivering education that we outlined above. We need an education system that is nimble and flexible, that adapts to challenges and seizes opportunities, that embraces and effectively utilizes cutting-edge technology not only in an emergency but as a matter of course, that rewards innovation and effectiveness. And if the crisis teaches us anything, it is that we must enable *all* parents, not only those who have their own resources to do so, to pursue the best educational options tailored to their children's needs.

Reforms that measure up to these principles will be systemic and transformative; reforms that do not will be superficial—a bandage on a deep wound. In the chapters that follow, we demonstrate why these principles are essential to the success of public education and illustrate how they translate into practice. To make a positive difference in the lives of American schoolchildren, to create a twenty-first-century educational system reflecting America's needs and capacity, requires courage, focus, imagination, and an unyielding focus on children.

CHAPTER 2

America's Dismal School System

The state of American public education can be measured at a fast-food cash register. Most transactions today are by credit card or electronic debit. But try using cash. Many high school students cannot compute change in their heads, even for the simplest transactions. If the young person at the register enters the incorrect amount, chaos ensues.

Our schools are not imparting the most basic, essential skills—skills that in past generations were taken for granted. The situation is even worse when it comes to the more advanced skills demanded of today's graduates. American schools are a bit like Congress. Most Americans think Congress is awful—but *their* elected representative is just fine. Same with education: most people think that American public schools are performing poorly overall, but *their* public school is pretty good.

They are right about the first part and usually wrong about the second. It is not just other people's schools that are performing so poorly; even many highly ranked schools in affluent communities fail to perform. As a whole, our K–12 education system falls far short in its essential mission of producing an educated citizenry that can both compete successfully in the world economy and participate effectively in our democracy. To generate the resolve necessary to make things better requires us first to acknowledge how bad the situation is and how we have repeatedly failed to embrace the most obvious solutions.

Failing America's Future

Americans seem generally aware of the dismal state of public education. For some, headlines during the COVID-19 crisis such as "15,000 L.A. High

Schoolers Are AWOL Online, 40,000 Fail to Check In Daily amid Coronavirus Closures" (*Los Angeles Times*) and "COVID-19 Outbreak Highlights Critical Gaps in School Emergency Preparedness" (Brookings) made them acutely aware.[1] A recent poll by Real Clear Opinion Research shows that less than one-third of Americans believe the public schools are highly performing on the goals they consider most important: instilling citizenship; protecting students from violence and physical harm; and preparing students to enter the workforce, to understand American history, to think critically, to vote, to be curious, to respect America, and to compete globally.[2] Another survey found that only 16 percent of Americans describe our K–12 STEM (science, technology, engineering, and math) education as the best in the world or above average; 46 percent consider it below average.[3] Fifty-five percent of Americans believe the quality of education today is worse than when they were students.[4] And they are pessimistic about future improvement: a significant majority believe that in twenty years, the American public school system will be average or below average; only 13 percent think it will provide a model of excellence for the world.[5]

But even as Americans recognize the poor state of American education as a whole, they generally believe the problem lies outside their own neighborhood: while only 19 percent of Americans give the nation's schools an A or B grade, 43 percent give their local schools those top grades, and 70 percent of parents grade their own kids' schools A or B.[6]

Is this perceived dichotomy correct? If so, how is it that schools overall are performing so badly when our own kids' schools are so good? Perhaps it is because many Americans attribute bad schools to poverty. After all, children from more affluent families typically go on to higher education and successful careers, so the schools they attend must be good—right?

Unfortunately, the reality is that while most schools in high-poverty areas are faring poorly, the system as a whole is underperforming, because most affluent schools are as well. This is best measured by comparing our student outcomes to those from other industrialized countries around the world. Our economic competitors are cleaning our clock, producing far more high school graduates per capita who are highly educated in math and science and equipped to compete and solve problems effectively in the twenty-first-century economy.

In this regard, perhaps one statistic more than any other illustrates the depth and gravity of our nation's education crisis: *in terms of math performance, the most impoverished 10 percent of students in Shanghai, China, outperform the top 10 percent most affluent US students.*[7]

If the poorest children in China are learning more math than the most advantaged students in the United States, our nation is in serious trouble. Over the past several decades, China has emerged as our greatest threat and adversary, economically, militarily, and politically. China threatens freedom not only for its own people but around the world. But its K–12 education system is far more effective than ours, and if that continues, its economy will quickly overtake America's.

Even countries that are not often considered serious competitors to the United States are educating their children more effectively. We cannot sustain our nation's position as the land of opportunity and the most powerful and productive nation in the world so long as we have a deficient education system.

We are able to objectively measure and compare educational performance primarily through two gold-standard tests. The first is the National Assessment of Educational Progress (NAEP), a congressionally mandated national exam administered by the National Center for Education Statistics that tests proficiency at various grade levels. Unlike state-administered tests, which differ greatly in content and quality, NAEP provides an apples-to-apples comparison of states and groups of students each year and over time.

At the international level, the gold-standard test is the Programme for International Student Assessment (PISA), created in the 1990s by the Organisation for Economic Co-operation and Development (OECD), which includes thirty-six industrialized nations (at time of writing), in an effort to promote reform. (We will not use many acronyms, we promise!) PISA does not ask students to replicate what they learned in class but rather tests them on their ability to creatively apply their learning in novel situations across subject-matter boundaries—precisely what the rapidly evolving twenty-first-century economy requires.[8] PISA not only allows international comparisons but also generates abundant data to show what works.

Unfortunately, both NAEP and PISA results show that despite massively increased financial investment and myriad reform measures, American educational performance has been stagnant for a very long time, and the system as a whole is stubbornly resistant to improvement.

Recent NAEP scores in math and reading show no overall national gains since 2015 (except in Florida, which is profiled later in this book).[9] Only about one-quarter of American high school seniors are proficient or advanced in math, and about 22 percent in science. By contrast, 40 percent scored "below basic" in those two critical subjects.[10] Think about that: nearly twice as many American students do not grasp the most basic elements of math and science as those who are proficient. The trend lines are ominous: the 2019 NAEP exam revealed that reading scores among fourth- and eighth-graders actually dropped from the 2017 exam.[11] And those scores may drop again given the precious time many students lost during the pandemic.

The situation may be even more bleak when it comes to history, geography, and civics. NAEP results released in 2020 found that fewer than one-quarter of eighth-graders scored proficient or above on any of the three exams. On all three, those scoring below basic—the bottom category—outnumbered those demonstrating proficiency. History was worst, with only 14 percent of students scoring proficient or above and 36 percent scoring below basic. Only 23 percent scored proficient or above on civics, an especially worrisome showing given that these youngsters will be voters in four years. Nor do the exams expect too much: among Catholic school students, twice as many scored proficient on history as those who scored below proficient, and four times as many in civics.[12] We cannot expect our constitutional republic to flourish if our students do not have a basic grasp of history and civics.

The NAEP results are unsurprising, as academic performance among seventeen-year-olds has essentially flatlined across all subjects since the 1970s, even as we have nearly tripled our nation's educational expenditures in inflation-adjusted dollars over the same period.[13]

The fact that we have not improved student performance in fifty years despite spending nearly three times as much is staggering. Such stagnation is "remarkably unusual," remarked Andrew J. Coulson, who served as a policy analyst for the Cato Institute. "In virtually every other field, productivity has risen over this period due to the adoption of countless technological advances," many of which "would seem ideally suited to facilitating learning." And yet even "surrounded by this torrent of progress," Coulson observed, "education has remained anchored to the riverbed, watching the rest of the world rush past it."[14]

One would think that fifty years of increasing expenditures, unaccompanied by any—much less commensurate—improvement in educational performance, would lead to systemic rather than superficial changes. But as Coulson aptly observed, K–12 education seems impervious to significant modernization, much less systemic change.

The picture looks no better in an international comparison, as US schools lag behind many of our international counterparts, which is a disastrous state of affairs in a global economy in which our kids are competing directly not only with each other but with young people across the world. Our fifteen-year-olds ranked twenty-fourth in science and reading and thirty-eighth in math among seventy-one countries participating in the recent PISA test. Among the thirty-five OECD countries at the time of the test, the United States ranked nineteenth in science and thirtieth in math. Putting that in perspective, *American fifteen-year-olds rank nearly last in math compared to their counterparts in the world's industrialized nations.* We are looking up at the likes of Vietnam, Slovenia, and Poland, not to mention direct economic competitors such as Japan, Canada, and South Korea (which score near the top).[15]

But wait, the apologists say: America has a much larger immigrant population for whom English is a second language, making our schools' job much tougher than in countries with more homogenous populations. It is not clear how much that is true any longer, as many countries, especially in Europe, have rapidly growing immigrant populations. But OECD takes such factors into account and finds no correlation between a country's share of students with immigrant backgrounds and overall performance.[16]

These shockingly poor educational outcomes bode disastrous consequences for America's future competitiveness and prosperity. America will need one million more STEM workers than it will graduate from college over the next decade.[17] Because our colleges are unable to produce sufficient numbers of proficient STEM graduates, owing to students' poor high school foundations, we either will have to import more foreign-born graduates or export the jobs to other countries—both of which we are doing.[18]

Indeed, because our K–12 school system is not up to the task, we are increasingly dependent on immigrants for our tech industry and national prosperity. Between 20 and 25 percent of our STEM workforce consists of immigrants, a proportion that has doubled since 1990, and they are more highly educated than their native-born counterparts. Nearly 40 percent of America's software engineers and over one-quarter of our computer programmers are foreign-born.[19] Immigrants account for more than half of our Nobel Prize winners since 1990, more than half of our patents, and half of all the new companies in Silicon Valley.[20] These trends will continue (assuming our immigration policies continue to allow skilled newcomers to enter our country) until our nation's schools grow capable of producing the skilled and creative workforce and entrepreneurs necessary to sustain our prosperity.

The Achievement Gap

The situation is most dire for low-income and minority youngsters. Americans can feel pride for much in our history, but we should feel shame over the fact that in the sixty-five years since the US Supreme Court proclaimed in *Brown v. Board of Education* that our schools must provide equal educational opportunities, we have not come close to making good on that sacred promise.

Measured in terms of grand social experiments, it is not for lack of trying. From the 1960s to the 1990s (and still continuing in some places even today), America attempted to integrate schools through massive forced busing schemes and other methods. The resulting flight to the suburbs by families of means left inner-city school districts heavily segregated and deprived them of their economic base. In states like New Jersey, California, and Missouri, courts ordered hefty spending increases in high-poverty schools, which barely moved the needle on academic progress. More recently, under the guise of affirmative action, we have pursued the strategy of adding points to students' test scores based on race and ethnicity when they apply for college, a cosmetic fix that ignores and does nothing to remedy the underlying failure of the system as a whole.

The racial academic gap that divides whites and Asian Americans from Blacks and Hispanics is a stubborn feature of American education. Researchers agree that the academic gap has persisted for fifty years. They disagree only on whether it has grown, with one Stanford researcher, Eric Hanushek, finding that the academic gap has not changed over the past half century, while another Stanford researcher, Sean Reardon, says it has grown by 40 percent.[21] Regardless, both agree that a gaping racial academic gap is a persistent feature of American K–12 education. It is a stain on America.

After a radio debate over racial preferences in the 1990s, I was picked up by an African immigrant cab driver who had been listening. He summed up the issue better than anyone I have ever heard: "They don't understand that the problem is not in college. The problem is in kindergarten."

CB

The magnitude of the racial academic gap can be measured in numerous ways. On the PISA international math and science exams, Hispanic American students score roughly the same as students in Serbia and Romania, while African American students score about the same as students in Kazakhstan and below the performance of students in Albania, even though those countries spend a fraction of the money we do on K–12 education.[22] Our schools are falling woefully short in preparing minority students to compete in a world economy. As educational analyst Dr. Matthew Ladner notes, "The high level of spending in American schools appears broadly ineffectual for students of color."[23]

Meanwhile, on the 2017 NAEP test, while 37 percent of all high school seniors scored proficient in reading and 23 percent in math—a pretty disastrous showing overall—Black students fared even worse: only 17 percent of Black seniors were proficient in reading and 7 percent in math.[24] Let us reiterate that: *fewer than one in fourteen African American high school seniors are proficient in math.* This is a disaster and makes a mockery of the guarantee of equal educational opportunities.

Among class of 2018 high school students who took the Scholastic Aptitude Test (SAT), the mean reading score for Black students was 483 (out of 800), eighty-three points below the mean white score. The mean math score for Black students was 463, ninety-four points below the mean score for white students. Placing those scores into perspective, only 21 percent of Black students who took the SAT met college and career readiness standards in both reading and math, compared to nearly 60 percent of white students. By contrast, nearly half of Black students did not meet the standards for either reading or math, compared to only 16 percent of white students.[25]

Those alarming numbers do not even take into account the fact that a disproportionate number of minority students fail to graduate from high school at all. While 91 percent of Asian American and 89 percent of white students graduate from high school, the percentages for Hispanics (80 percent), Blacks (78 percent), and Native Americans (72 percent) are considerably lower.[26] Those numbers are significantly worse for inner-city students.[27] Dropping out of school has lifetime consequences: the average earnings of a high school dropout are only $600 per week.[28]

Nor is the trajectory hopeful. Based on the most recent NAEP and PISA data, the *New York Times* reports that the academic gap is actually widening: while the top quarter of American students have improved their academic performance since 2012, performance among the bottom 10 percent of students has declined.[29] The PISA exam revealed that about one-fifth of American fifteen-year-olds scored so low that they were not reading at the level expected of ten-year-olds.[30]

Putting all of these numbers together makes for a grim prognosis: *a Black child in the United States has less than a one-in-six chance of graduating from high school ready for a career or college.* Those stark disparities translate into diminished college admissions and graduation, job prospects, income, wealth creation, and mobility. It is a national catastrophe.

Many minority and low-income parents recognize that the schools to which their children are consigned are not good. While more than half of all

Americans in high- or upper-middle-income areas award their schools an A or B grade, only one-third of Blacks and lower-income families of all races rate their schools that high.[31] Despite other gains we have made in racial equality over the last half century, so long as our nation is still mired in a state of educational apartheid, we will not have anything approaching truly equal opportunity.

What is especially distressing about these unequal educational opportunities is that we know how to do better for low-income children and students of color. For instance, the national charter schools of the Knowledge Is Power Program (KIPP) generate excellent outcomes for a student population that is 95 percent Black or Hispanic and 89 percent eligible for free and reduced lunch.[32] The public schools of Newark, New Jersey, previously among the nation's worst, boosted graduation rates by one-quarter and significantly improved reading scores by closing failing public schools, expanding high-performing charter schools, and introducing teacher merit pay.[33] (Unfortunately, in response to special-interest pressure, many of those policies have been reversed.)[34] And as we recount in chapter 10, Florida has greatly narrowed the academic gap while boosting test scores among all demographic groups through an array of systemic reforms.

What prevents public schools from providing high-quality educational opportunities to the most disadvantaged students? Three decades ago, education researchers John Chubb and Terry Moe set out to discover why inner-city public schools are so much worse than suburban public schools and inner-city private schools. Their findings, published by the Brookings Institution, still resonate today. Chubb and Moe found that as political institutions, schools tend to respond more to special interests than to those they educate. That situation is exacerbated in inner-city public schools, which are characterized by massive, impenetrable, and impersonal bureaucracies. And whereas dissatisfied families in the suburbs can move, and unhappy families whose children are enrolled in public schools can send them to private schools, most inner-city public school students have no choice. As a result, low-income families have far less power to influence their children's education, and those who hold the reins of power have little incentive to respond to their needs.[35]

Any effort to redress unequal educational opportunities must eliminate that power disparity, providing to low-income parents the same ability to secure high-quality education for their children as more affluent parents.

 When Bill and Hillary Clinton opted to send their daughter to an elite private school when they were in the White House, Wisconsin state representative Polly Williams, an African American Democrat and architect of the Milwaukee Parental Choice Program, quipped that "Bill and Hillary Clinton should not be the only people who live in public housing who get to send their kid to private school."

The Most Common Solution Isn't the Right One

Many people think they know what's wrong with American K–12 public education: we don't spend enough on it.

That pervasive notion is testament to the amazing success of those who defend or benefit from the status quo in convincing people that we need to give the system more money—preferably with no strings attached.

It is hard to imagine that reaction to any other poor-quality product. When a car manufacturer rolls a low-quality product off the assembly line, we don't buy it. When that happens, the company has an incentive to improve the product. What we emphatically do not do in that situation is to insist on paying more money for the failing product in the hope that the car company will eventually improve the product. Yet that is exactly what many Americans think we should do when it comes to our public schools. Certainly spending more money is much easier than fixing what is wrong.

True improvement requires us to challenge this conventional wisdom. America already spends more on K–12 public education than almost every other country—with much less to show for it. As we will discuss, increasing spending beyond a certain level does not correlate with improved results. When we do increase funding, most of the money goes to bureaucracy and pension liabilities rather than to children and the highest-performing teachers. The bottom line is that K–12 public education is already well funded, but the dollars are often spent unwisely—and those dollars are not controlled by the people who have the greatest stake in achieving success.

Still, over one-quarter of Americans believe that the biggest problem facing public schools is not enough money.[36] Nearly half say that school spending should increase by at least 7 percent.[37] Two-thirds say teachers are underpaid—the highest percentage expressing that view since polling on the question began in 1969.[38] Those views are fueled by recent teacher strikes, lobbying campaigns, and ballot measures that equate support for public education with increased funding. The message is hard to resist and certainly daunting to argue against: if you care about kids, you must support more money for the school system.

That message is startlingly effective in making people think we are not spending nearly enough. Yet the truth is that Americans do not understand how much we spend in the first place. The median American estimated that we spent $5,000 per student in 2019, while the median teacher estimated that we spent $4,000 per student. Seventy-nine percent of Americans believe we spend less than $10,000 a year on average per pupil. In fact, the national average for 2019 was $12,201 per pupil.[39] The general public also thinks teachers make about $18,000 less than they actually do, on average. When provided with the real figures, public support for more school funding and teacher pay raises drops drastically.[40]

Even crediting the argument that we don't spend enough on K–12 education, the problem is that proposed funding increases are almost never linked to systemic reform or even to basic performance. And the dollars themselves are rarely targeted to the intended destinations: teachers, kids, and classrooms. Borrowing a term the left often uses, we might characterize the process as trickle-down spending: showering increased resources on the system as a whole, in the doubtful hope that they will eventually trickle down to the intended beneficiaries.

Among OECD countries, many of which are blowing our doors off, performance-wise, K–12 spending averages less than $11,000 annually per student. Yet the average American student trails the typical OECD student in math by a half year. The gap is even larger with students from South Korea and Finland (three years!), yet Finland spends about $11,000 per student and South Korea spends less than $10,000.[41]

If the United States spends so much more, why are many countries that spend less money doing better?

The most immediate answer is a bit counterintuitive: in K–12 education, cost generally does not equal quality. Extrapolating data over decades from dozens of countries, OECD's Andreas Schleicher, a German statistician and education researcher who created the PISA exam, found that for countries spending $5,000 or less annually per pupil, a strong correlation exists between the amount of spending and student performance. However, above that minimum amount, *the correlation between the amount of spending and student performance is nonexistent.* Indeed, Luxembourg spends four times as much annually per student as Hungary, but their educational results are roughly equal.[42]

The same has been true within the United States since the 1970s. We have nearly tripled the amount of K–12 education spending in constant dollars with no academic performance gains among high school seniors.[43] As the Cato Institute's Andrew Coulson found, based on forty years of data, "There is essentially no link between state education spending (which has exploded) and the performance of students at the end of high school (which has generally stagnated or declined)."[44] Schleicher's observation on this point is one of the most important insights for meaningful education reform: "In short, success is not just about how much money is spent, but about how that money is spent."[45]

In coming chapters, we explore ways to spend our educational resources more wisely, paying high-performing teachers more, spending less on bureaucracy, and giving far greater control to educational producers and consumers. Just as we do in private enterprise, and even in other public endeavors, we must insist upon a positive return on investment. That is the essence of the structural change necessary to build a twenty-first-century educational system.

Facing Reality

How is it that the greatest, most creative, most productive nation in the world ended up with such a lousy K–12 educational system, despite spending more per capita than nearly any other country? Clearly, we know how to create an excellent educational system: our postsecondary colleges and universities, while not without serious flaws, remain the world's envy, attracting millions of the best and brightest students from all around the globe. By contrast, there is probably not a single industrialized country that would trade its K–12 educational system for ours, certainly not given its high costs.

Explanations abound. In a nation whose mindset is more individualistic and antibureaucratic than any other, America's K–12 educational system is one of the most bureaucratic and least personalized in the free world. Unlike almost every other important service in America (including postsecondary education), K–12 education is largely bereft of meaningful competition and choice, and the dollars generally flow directly from the government to the bureaucracy that controls the service providers, rather than from consumers to the service providers themselves. Unlike in the vast majority of American enterprises, few people in the system are held accountable or rewarded for performance. Those with the greatest stake in successful outcomes tend to have the least power to achieve them. And the system has powerful built-in defense mechanisms against change.

The OECD's Schleicher places the challenge in context: "Our current schools were created in the industrial age, when the prevailing norms were standardization and compliance, and when it was both effective and efficient to educate children in batches and to train teachers once for their entire lives." In this system, the "curricula that spelled out what students should learn were designed at the top of the pyramid, then translated into instructional material, teacher education and learning environments, often through multiple levels of government, until they reached and were implemented by individual teachers in the classroom."[46]

That means that the people with the greatest stake in successful educational outcomes—parents, teachers, and principals—often have the least influence. Indeed, among OECD nations, *the United States ranks eighteenth in school autonomy—lower than Russia!*[47] We desperately need to change that equation; it starts with giving more power to consumers and producers rather than bureaucrats and middlemen.

Little has changed from the educational structure that we inherited from the nineteenth century. As Andrew J. Coulson remarked, this has been "a long time for a field to stand outside of history," suggesting that "perhaps it's time to ask if there are inherent features in our approach to schooling that prevent it from experiencing the progress typical in other fields."[48]

Indeed, given the many ambitious, well-intentioned efforts at reform over the past several decades and the vast advances we have witnessed in almost every other part of our lives, how can we still have such an antiquated K–12 education system? The answer is sobering: powerful interests who have a vested stake in preserving the status quo have both the incentive and the ability to thwart meaningful change. As OECD's Schleicher observes, "The vast structure of established, usually public, providers means that there are extensive special interests. As a result, the status quo has many protectors—stakeholders in education who stand to lose a degree of power or influence if changes are made."[49]

Therefore, Schleicher urges, "To transform schooling at scale, we need not just a radical, alternative vision of what's possible, but also smart strategies and effective institutions." Transformative reform "requires a carefully crafted enabling environment that can unleash teachers' and schools' ingenuity and build capacity for change."[50] The American K–12 education system is so underperforming and antiquated that we should never reject a possible solution because it is too ambitious; we should always ask whether it is ambitious enough.

Americans are angry about a lot of things. Remarkably, most do not seem angry over the pathetic state of K–12 education and the abysmal return on their tax dollars. Given our massive public investment, the stubborn resistance to reform, and the urgent necessity for improvement, especially for those who need better educational opportunities the most, Americans should be white-hot angry about the educational status quo. Summoning the vast tools available to them and drawing upon our core principles and experience, Americans can solve anything. We can and must solve the education crisis.

CHAPTER 3

Eliminating the Middleman

Returning to the thought experiment with which we began the book: if we were designing a twenty-first-century school system from scratch, without preconceptions, who among us would organize the control and delivery of K–12 education through the school districts we have today?

American public education is subject to a triple bureaucracy: federal, state, and local (plus additional bureaucracy in the schools themselves). Like most bureaucracies, the educational variety absorbs precious resources without contributing commensurately to educational outcomes. As we highlighted in the previous chapter, though education funding has steadily increased, we have used an ever-larger share of those dollars to purchase added bureaucracy without getting improved quality in return.

The emphasis on growing central bureaucracy rather than concentrating more resources in the classroom occurs because administrators rather than consumers and service providers decide how most education dollars are spent, and those administrators are beholden to political officials rather than the consumers they serve—an equation that absolutely must change if we are to improve education.

Education across America is funded primarily by the states. Most state money is distributed to school districts rather than to schools or families. The lion's share of the remaining funding comes in most states from local property taxes. In turn, most decisions on how the money is spent are made by school districts.

That this remains so in the twenty-first century is in sharp contrast to the trend in nearly every aspect of American life toward "disintermediation"—that is, the removal of middlemen standing between producers and consumers.

Disintermediation generally reduces costs and makes products and services more responsive to consumer needs and desires.

Dramatic advances in education technology have made it possible to customize education for individual students and provide it at a fraction of the cost of standardized institutional delivery. One case in point involves Ivy League colleges offering free online college courses.[1] Disintermediation would allow greater consumer sovereignty and personalized service delivery in K-12 education. The main obstacle preventing this from happening is the delivery of public education through school districts. Despite the proliferation of charter schools and other forms of school choice, which generally operate outside centralized government bureaucracies, the delivery of public education remains subject to monopoly school district control.

Local Leviathans

Standing between those who produce and consume education are state and local bureaucracies, which siphon significant funding from the educational enterprise. The districts in turn have double governance: elected or appointed boards composed of political officials, and administrative governance consisting of superintendents and other administrative officials. School board members are often uncompensated, work very long hours, and receive few thanks. We hope that any reform structure will provide abundant opportunities for their gainful civic energy, such as boards of individual schools. On the other hand, administrative officials are often lavishly compensated. Superintendents often stay in their districts only a short period of time, either being fired (typically with generous severance packages) or moving to other districts. The data show that nearly a quarter of district superintendents leave before serving three years, and the majority leave before serving for six.[2] Superintendent churn, like most unfortunate trends in education, occurs more in districts serving low-income and minority students. Strong, reform-minded superintendents can bring positive, transformative changes to school districts (if they are not stymied by bureaucracy)—although the results are often overstated, creating a false bandwagon effect.[3] But if we had far fewer superintendents and other administrative officials, we would have lots more dollars to spend on instruction.

Bureaucracy does not advance the educational enterprise. In most cases, it actually stifles it, removing decision making from school-level actors and inflating costs; hence more spending may portend not only diminishing returns but even negative returns.

Our nation, which ordinarily considers itself bureaucracy averse, nonetheless spends much more on administration than other OECD countries. Even a decade ago, the United States spent 54.8 cents of every school operating dollar on teachers, compared to an average of 63.8 cents per dollar for other OECD countries. Over a quarter of this same dollar in the United States was spent on administrators and support personnel, compared to 14.9 cents per dollar elsewhere in the OECD.[4] In other words, we spent nearly twice as much on educational bureaucracy than our international competitors.

A recent article by economics professor Dr. Benjamin Scafidi illustrates this phenomenon. Between 1950 and 2015, the number of K–12 students doubled. The number of teachers increased by 243 percent, greatly eclipsing student population growth. But that increase is dwarfed by administrative and other nonteaching staff, which grew by 709 percent during the same period. In other words, *over the past sixty-five years, the number of administrative and support personnel has grown more than seven times faster than the number of students.*[5]

This trend has persisted in recent years. Between 1992 and 2014, K–12 spending increased by 27 percent in inflation-adjusted dollars. The number of students increased during that same period by 19 percent, much less than spending growth. The number of teachers increased by 28 percent, while the number of other staff grew by a massive 45 percent—more than twice the rate of student population growth.[6]

To put the trend in a different perspective, in 1950 the ratio of students to teachers in the public education system was 27.5 to one and the ratio of students to nonteachers was 65 to one. In 1992, the student-to-teacher ratio was 17.3 to one and the student-to-nonteacher ratio was 19.8 to one. Today, there are one teacher and one nonteacher for every 16 students.[7] The resource diversion from classroom to bureaucracy increases relentlessly. Since 2012, the growth in the number of administrators has been three times the growth in the number of teachers.[8] Between 1992 and 2014, while per-pupil spending increased by nearly one-third, average teacher salaries actually declined by nearly $1,000.[9] Instead, the spending spike financed the decades-long surge in nonteaching personnel. In Newark, New Jersey, administration absorbs more than half of the more than $20,000 spent on each student.[10] In California, school administration has grown by 50 percent since 1992, outpacing student growth by more than two to one. Had administration increased at the same rate as the student population, the state education budget would have been $3 billion dollars smaller[11]—leaving money that could have been used to reduce pension liabilities, increase teacher salaries, reduce taxes, or provide alternative educational options.

Scafidi puts this resource diversion in stark national perspective: *between 1992 and 2015, if the growth in nonteaching personnel had been no greater than the growth in the number of students, we would have saved $805 billion—enough to give every teacher an $11,100 pay raise or provide $8,000 education savings accounts to 4.36 million students* (see chapters 5 and 6).

This is a staggering misprioritization of precious resources. As Scafidi observes, "It is likely that few would be concerned about this . . . dramatic change in the composition of the workforce and the associated added workplace costs if outcomes for public school students had increased during these decades."[12] But no such improvement has occurred: as the preceding chapter demonstrates, educational performance has flatlined for nearly half a century. Providing large salaries to an ever-growing number of school district administrators has not boosted performance, but it has diverted dollars from where they could make a difference.

School districts as currently constituted are a relic of the nineteenth century. School district boundaries drawn one hundred or more years ago often make little sense today. In Arizona, elementary school district boundaries are often not contiguous with municipal boundaries, and elementary and high school district lines are sometimes not contiguous with one another. Some school districts, such as those in New York, Chicago, and Los Angeles, among many others, are so massive that individual parents, teachers, and principals cannot possibly have a meaningful voice in the educational process, or even over their own children's circumstances. Others are so tiny that it is impossible to justify the cost of their duplicative functions and bureaucracies.

OECD's Andreas Schleicher identifies school districts as a major source of American overregulation of education. "American schools tend to get much more direction from the local district office than is the case in many other countries," he observes. "In that sense, the United States may have traded one form of centralized bureaucracy for another."[13] Or, more precisely, we have created multiple layers of bureaucracy, which impedes greatly our ability to innovate and improve. "The changes in our societies have greatly outpaced the structural capacity of our current governance systems to respond," Schleicher warns. "Top-down governance through layers of administrative structure is no longer working."[14]

School districts are defended by nostalgic conservatives who extol the virtues of local control. Unquestionably, in many communities, the public schools are the focus of enormous civic energy. Much if not most of that civic engagement is directed toward individual schools rather than the district as a whole, which is of course how it should be, because parental involvement in their children's schools aids the educational enterprise in innumerable ways.

But too often, "local control" translates into excessive influence by special-interest groups, including unions, who turn out in large numbers for small-turnout elections that are typically not aligned with general elections. This phenomenon was forecast by America's founders, who explained that the smaller the government, the more susceptible it is to capture by self-focused special interests.[15] If we want true local control, we need to take it an important further step: power over education should not be vested in a political unit but devolved to the school level, where decisions can be made by principals, teachers, and families.

Engines of Inequality

School districts are also the main cause of educational inequality. District boundary lines often artificially separate white from Black, rich from poor.

Even though the states are constitutionally obligated to provide education, children's residence determines in large part the quality of the public education they can obtain.

"The whole of American education works this way," charges Kevin Carey, who directs education policy for the New America think tank. Our educational system is divided "by tens of thousands of borders that citizens are forbidden to cross under threat of incarceration—parents who enroll their children in nearby school districts face fines and even jail." The school district "walls have been there so long," Carey observes, "that people largely just accept them as an unalterable part of the landscape, like cliffs and rivers that can be built around and occasionally bridged at great expense, but never truly changed."[16]

I remember as a youngster when my suburban New Jersey school district hired a detective to follow students home to make sure their parents weren't lying about their home addresses to get their kids into the schools. In Chicago, where I represented low-income families, it was an open secret that poor parents would exercise "school choice" by giving their kids a relative's address to get them into a school other than the one for which they were zoned, although they had to break the law to do so.

In states that rely in significant part on property taxes, huge disparities often exist between affluent and poorer school districts. States such as New Jersey have responded by dramatically increasing school funding and redistributing it to poorer school districts, typically with little educational effect. Moreover, wealthier school districts often raise their own spending in response, thereby creating new inequalities and contributing to a never-ending cycle of spending increases without accompanying improvement.

Most important, school district boundaries often provide impenetrable barriers to educational access. Affluent families exercise public school choice by moving to districts with higher property taxes and better schools, while families who lack the means to do so are trapped in failing school districts.

By contrast, in states like Arizona that have open public school enrollment, schools and districts compete for students and the resources they command by providing programs or services families want. Families can vote with their feet: in Maricopa County, for instance, 47 percent of students are attending a school other than the one for which they are zoned, and 37 percent attend schools outside their districts.[17] But even then, schools must give preference to students zoned for them, creating waiting lists for the best schools and leaving many children without adequate public-sector opportunities.

Taming the Behemoth

Recognizing the inefficiencies of school districts and the arbitrary nature of district boundaries that were often drawn over a century ago, some reformers have proposed consolidating school districts. Consolidation, they argue, would reduce inequality and inefficiency. Unquestionably, fewer and larger school districts could theoretically capture greater economies of scale. But so long as they remain bloated bureaucracies and political institutions subject to special-interest capture, consolidated school districts could worsen the status quo by making the locus of power and decision making even more remote from education providers and consumers. And even consolidation is fiercely resisted by school districts and those whose livelihoods depend on them. If reformers are going to attempt such a heavy political lift, they should instead pursue change that will make a much bigger difference.

Rather than making school districts larger, we should ask whether they are necessary at all—and if they are, whether it would make sense to dramatically change their roles. Imagine the systemic change that would occur if schools received funding based primarily on decisions by families to spend their education funding there—and if the schools themselves, through principals and teachers, could decide how those resources are used. And imagine how many more resources schools would have if eighty or ninety cents of every education dollar, rather than fifty or sixty cents, were directed to them. We believe *every* public school should have the power to craft educational programs and strategies to meet the needs of their students, the authority to decide how resources are allocated, and accountability for results. This is the vision we present in the next chapter.

What about the vital services that school districts provide, such as transportation, recruitment and hiring, payroll and benefits, special services for students with disabilities, and so on? Instead of monopoly provision of crucial services at great cost through a politicized central bureaucracy, whose services are duplicated by the district next door, the state could provide such services directly or through regional service providers, or schools could purchase them competitively through private vendors.

Ideally, schools, rather than self-interested administrators, should decide how much bureaucracy they need. If services were competitively bid, or at least produced by nonpolitical entities designed to provide those services, schools could prioritize their needs and allocate their resources accordingly. In this regard, district schools should draw upon the experience of charter schools, whose statewide associations often provide pooled insurance and other services and which often join together to create economies of scale. Service providers compete by price and quality to attract their business. Charter schools also often form networks, pooling their resources to purchase special-education services, recruit teachers, develop and implement nondiscrimination policies and procedures, and so forth.

While entities like these could offer the important *services* currently provided by school districts, they would not operate as *political* units. They would have only such personnel as were necessary to add value to the schools. And the schools would have the option to change providers if they could find better or less expensive services. The savings reaped from eliminating unnecessary bureaucracy would pass to the schools themselves, which—subject to state governance and oversight—would have the power to decide how to expend resources.

Eliminating school districts or redefining their role would also remove a major obstacle to education reform. School districts and school board associations are powerful players in state capitals, often leveraging tax dollars to advance their interests. They typically oppose any efforts to reduce their power and are backed by administrators, who have their own lobbying associations. In Texas, for instance, rural school districts, which are often the biggest employers in their communities, have for decades successfully resisted most systemic reform efforts in a state that is in other areas a leader in market-oriented reforms.

This systemic change poses a test of our commitment to serious reform: Are we more concerned about children or the adults who are employed by the system? Do we really need four times more administrators per student than we had in 1950? By keeping the current school district system in place, we can expect that the proportion of nonteachers in our K–12 school system—which in 2015 caught up with the number of teachers[18]—will continue to grow. And we can continue to expect that an ever-growing bureaucracy will do nothing to improve educational quality or outcomes.

Abolishing school districts and attendance zones would be fiercely resisted by the powerful entities benefiting from the status quo—not only those whose livelihoods depend on school districts (though most who provide valuable services will remain in great demand) but also those who are on the preferred side of the attendance zones. Wealthy and middle-class families work hard and invest heavily to make sure they live in desirable school districts—and who can blame them? For that reason, it is crucial that unlike coercive reform strategies of the past, such as forced busing and district rezoning, which were fiercely resisted because they redistributed opportunities, our efforts must be focused on improving quality and expanding opportunities.

"If we look at the world as having a fixed sum of desirable schools, we should not be surprised if the wealthy hoard access to them," urges education policy analyst Dr. Matthew Ladner, nor that they would fiercely guard their advantage with the powerful political clout at their disposal. But if "we expand the supply of desirable schools and thus weaken the link between zip code and schooling, and if we give communities of all types more options to specialized schooling, we have a chance."[19]

And imagine the odd-couple coalition that potentially could be assembled to get it done: teachers and principals, who would reap greater control over resources and educational programs; parents, who would have more influence over their children's education; taxpayers, who might see savings or at least greater return on investment; and liberal reformers, who correctly identify school district boundaries and property-tax-based school financing as sources of inequality.

Necessarily, in such a system, the state would have to assume the primary if not exclusive role over education finance. That ultimately makes sense given that in most if not all state constitutions, state government is assigned the responsibility of providing K–12 education. The trend in recent years has been in that direction anyway, largely as a result of educational equity lawsuits that have targeted property-tax-based education funding. Of course, when the state assumes a greater role in education finance, one result should be proportionately reduced local property taxes. Overall, the transition from school districts to school-based control should result in devoting a far higher share of education funding to classrooms (and, in states that provide for it through legislation, parental choice).

In a school-based rather than district-based system of education, the state would also have to take a more proactive role in ensuring that schools meet state standards and that all students have access to high-quality opportunities. Several states have taken over school districts when they have failed to meet their responsibilities; in Florida, the state intervenes when a school receives a failing grade on the state report card (see chapter 10). Expanded autonomy necessarily entails greater accountability, and the state should take strong remedial action—including replacing management—when schools fail to measure up. We will discuss in greater detail how this structure would operate in coming chapters.

Where abolishing school districts proves impossible, reformers should still push to transfer greater autonomy to individual schools. By making schools rather than districts the destination for state funding, by giving principals greater control over personnel and educational programming, and by empowering teachers and parents to play a greater role in educational governance, schools can be more nimble, responsive, and productive.

Even in the best-case scenario, school districts and attendance zones will not wither away quickly or easily. In the meantime, it is imperative to expand, as best we can, the opportunities available to disadvantaged students whose families cannot buy homes in more affluent districts. This does not mean sending more money to those school districts with no strings attached—after all, many districts with large low-income student populations already receive higher funding and often produce the worst academic results.

Rather, it means giving families of modest means the same opportunity that more affluent parents possess, for everyone has school choice except the poor. As Dr. Ladner puts it, we should focus on "creating school options where access is delightfully independent of the zip code in which a child lives: magnet schools, charter schools, private choice programs and home schooling." Although a "frontal assault on purchased privilege may seem tempting," Ladner acknowledges, it is doomed to failure. "Zip code assignment to schools, however, is a practice which does not merit anyone's support."[20]

In a century in which consumers are increasingly empowered to make crucial decisions without government-assigned intermediaries, the time is overdue to reconsider the role played by school districts, as well as the awesome power they wield and the resources they control. Creating a twenty-first-century American education system requires giving far greater control to those with the greatest stake in successful outcomes: service providers and consumers. We need to replace top-down governance with bottom-up decision making. The single most important change we can make in the public school arena is to remove the middleman between educational producers and consumers.

CHAPTER 4

Decentralizing Education

If we can eliminate or reduce the power of central school district bureaucracies over individual schools, their funding, and their governance, the realm of the possible expands greatly in terms of what public schools can accomplish. In this new system, public schools will be much more autonomous: they will be responsible to the state in terms of educational basics and quality, responsible to parents and students whom they need to attract and retain, and largely free to adopt strategies and allocate resources to fulfill those responsibilities as they deem best.

We call this new model "community schools," for the schools themselves would be self-contained educational communities even as they are part of the bigger system of K–12 public education. To say the transition from highly regimented district schools to semiautonomous community schools would constitute a sea change in the delivery of K–12 education is a great understatement.

In this chapter, we examine the ultimate in decentralization: giving families control over how their educational resources are spent. Later we explore how disruptive innovation can make all schools and learning more effective. But first we address a core issue that proponents of greater choice and competition too often glide over: how should the public schools that, at least for the foreseeable future, will serve the vast majority of American students be organized in a more efficient, effective, streamlined, deregulated, decentralized environment?

The Lesson of Charter Schools

Fortunately, we do not have to speculate very much, because over the past few decades we have experienced a major educational innovation that demonstrates both progress and promise: charter schools.

In our view, charter schools provide not only crucial educational alternatives but also lessons, based on both successes and failures, for what unshackled public schools could and should look like. Some opponents of charter schools or their expansion argue that they should be governed just like regular public schools: regulated by public officials down to the paper clip. What if, instead, we turn that equation around and argue that regular public schools should be given much the same flexibility as charter schools?

Charter schools are independently operated public schools. Applicable rules vary widely from state to state (and some states do not have charter schools at all). Typically, they are run by nonprofit organizations, sometimes by for-profit entities. The sponsors are awarded charters by the state or other chartering entities (such as school districts or public universities) for a set period of time. In exchange for meeting performance standards, charter schools are freed from many of the state and local dictates that apply to regular public schools, including (crucially) teacher hiring and compensation. Student performance is monitored, and poor-performing charter schools can be closed or not have their charters renewed. Charter schools receive state funding based on the number of students who enroll, and they must cover their own facility costs out of their budgets; for that reason, charter schools usually receive significantly fewer public resources than other public schools. Like other public schools, charter schools are required to comply with civil rights laws and other educational guarantees. But within the general state and federal governing framework, they have great flexibility that traditional public schools lack.

The following are crucial defining characteristics that help make many charter schools dynamic and effective. Few traditional public schools today share those characteristics, but public schools in the future should:

- Charter schools are mission driven and largely self-governed, including control over their own budgets.
- Although they must teach the state's required basic curriculum, they are free to offer a specialized focus such as STEM, fine arts, great books, intensive math and English for students behind grade level, or language immersion.
- They accept students on a random selection basis without regard to where they live, usually with a lottery when applicants outnumber spaces.

- They are funded on a per-capita basis based on the number of students who choose to attend.
- They hire and fire their own teachers, generally prioritizing subject-matter expertise rather than teaching credentials.
- They compensate teachers based on performance and expertise.
- They often organize consortia for insurance, transportation, children with disabilities, and other services.
- They can be shut down if they do not follow their governing charters or fulfill performance targets.
- They can be unionized or not.

Imagine how much more effective public schools could be if they were freed from rigid governance and programmatic requirements.

We envision a system of community schools sponsored and funded by the state and subject to the state's baseline requirements for testing and performance supervision. Unlike in charter schools, capital needs would be met by the state. Noncapital funding would be driven by student demand, with educationally disadvantaged and special-needs students receiving greater per-student amounts. In accordance with state constitutional guarantees, the state would ensure that every child has access to community schools. Educators and families could petition the state to open new schools. Most important, the state could close or reorganize poor-performing schools. (Florida does exactly that, as we describe in chapter 10.) But like charter schools, they would be self-managed by independent boards of directors.

Let's take a look at the charter school experience to see how lessons learned can be applied to public schools to make them more flexible, autonomous, responsive, and effective.

The first charter school law was passed in Minnesota in 1991. Today, only three decades later, forty-three states and the District of Columbia have charter schools. Growth has been explosive: more than three million students now attend public charter schools, roughly 6 percent of the nation's K–12 population, and more than six times as many as were attending charter schools at the beginning of the century. Since 2000, charter schools have experienced nearly four times the student growth as traditional public schools (2.6 million net growth among charter students compared to about 700,000 in traditional public schools).[1] Those numbers are astounding given that there are far fewer charter schools than district schools available to students, and some states still do not offer charter schools at all.

Charter schools are both a red- and blue-state phenomenon. California has the highest number of charter school students (603,000 students, 10 percent of the total student population). The District of Columbia has the highest percentage of its students enrolled in charter schools (44 percent), followed by Arizona (17 percent).[2]

Notably, and contrary to stereotypes promoted by their opponents, charter schools overall serve a higher proportion of minority and low-income students than traditional public schools. Fewer than one-third of charter school students are white. One-quarter are African American. More charter school students are Hispanic than either white or Black. Indeed, the percentage of charter school students who are Hispanic has increased dramatically, from 16 percent in 2000 to 33 percent in 2016. At the same time, 34 percent of charter school students are in schools with high-poverty populations, compared to 24 percent of traditional public school students.[3]

The fact that low-income and minority students are pouring into charter schools (and other school choice programs) underscores the imperative to protect and expand those options as well as the need to cultivate more flexible public schools that can effectively serve such students' needs.

Despite being more likely to serve students with special challenges, charter schools are often highly successful. Nationally, charter school students are more likely to graduate from high school, attend college, and earn high salaries than their traditional public school peers. A Stanford University study of charter schools in forty-one urban areas across twenty-two states found that their students experienced annual academic gains relative to their district school peers equivalent to an extra forty days of learning for math and twenty-eight days in reading. The gains are most pronounced among Black and Hispanic students.[4] Although charter schools receive an average of nearly $6,000 less per student than traditional public schools, their academic return on taxpayer investment is far greater for each dollar they receive.[5] Academic results are compounded by the fact that charter school graduates are more likely to persist in college and to have greater average earnings by their mid-twenties.[6]

Charter schools are a highly diverse phenomenon. Sixty-five percent are freestanding, self-managed schools. The other 35 percent are run by management organizations; among those, two-thirds are nonprofits.[7]

Success stories abound among innovative charter schools, which often target populations that fall through the cracks in traditional public schools, such as high-poverty students, English-as-a-second-language students, high school dropouts, and disabled children. Many have replicated their success by opening additional schools.

The largest charter school network is the Knowledge Is Power Program (KIPP), with 242 schools across the nation serving an overwhelmingly low-income and minority student population: 95 percent are Black or Hispanic, and 88 percent are eligible for free or reduced lunches.[8] KIPP emphasizes high expectations, character development, highly effective teachers and leaders, a safe and nurturing environment, and college readiness.[9] The results blow the doors off paternalistic notions that low-income children cannot succeed and the argument that schools fail because the children can't learn. Among many other positive results, a 2019 Mathematica study found that attending a KIPP middle school could close the racial gap in college attendance—that is, minority students who attend KIPP schools in their adolescent years attend college at the same rates as white students.[10]

In New York City, the Success Academy, a charter school network founded by former Democratic city council member Eva Moskowitz, has delivered (as its name promises) great academic success to its largely low-income student population. In 2017, its eighth-graders sat for the Algebra I Regents Examination for the first time—and 99 percent passed, compared to 62 percent of students in the city's traditional public schools. The Success students not only passed but excelled, with 93 percent of the eighth-graders demonstrating college readiness. Those results, says Moskowitz, "demonstrate that low-income children of color can achieve at the highest level."[11]

Another huge success story is BASIS Charter Schools, with twenty-seven elementary and high schools enrolling nearly one hundred thousand students in states that are friendly to charters as well as the District of Columbia.[12] Founders and economists Michael and Olga Block realized that American students were being held to low expectations, so they crafted a more rigorous model focusing on STEM and college-level coursework. The BASIS curriculum is widely regarded as one of the most academically rigorous high school programs in the world.[13] Students are challenged to reach the highest international benchmarks, and teachers instill a sense of responsibility for learning in students while also providing constant support. At BASIS, students complete a rigorous, accelerated course of study—with Advanced Placement (AP) classes at the forefront. In most American high schools, AP classes are taught at the eleventh-grade level and above, but BASIS offers them to students at a much younger age. Students are required to take, and pass, six AP exams to graduate from BASIS. Yet the school reports that many students take more than ten, starting in middle school—boasting an 86 percent pass rate in 2017.[14] A nod to their founders, the BASIS curriculum also mandates that eighth-graders take an entire year of economics.

The results are stupendous. Seven BASIS high schools rank in the *U.S. News & World Report*'s top fifty public high schools in the United States, and they swept eight of the top ten public high school ratings in Arizona, including all of the top seven.[15] BASIS also earned three of the top ten spots on the *Washington Post*'s 2017 list of America's most challenging high schools.[16] Most important, on the international PISA exam, *BASIS students outscore students from the top countries—Singapore, China, Japan, Hong Kong—by wide margins in math, reading, and science.*[17]

As BASIS students take courses earlier than peers at other high schools, they are allowed to graduate after eleventh grade to enroll in college. Yet many students remain for their twelfth-grade year, which looks nothing like their prior years of high school. Seniors take an interactive college counseling workshop and a number of capstone courses, either through the AP Capstone program or BASIS's own version. Comparable to 200- or 300-level college courses, these capstone experiences can profoundly impact students' success in college and future careers. Finally, at the end of twelfth grade, BASIS students conduct an intensive, off-campus research program related to their academic and career goals.[18] Teaming up with corporations, entrepreneurs, agencies, and researchers across fields nationally and internationally to complete the project, students build intellectual curiosity, real-world knowledge, and a network. BASIS Phoenix students have completed projects titled "Creating Better Tests for Infectious Diseases" and "Inclusivity in Entrepreneurship: How Network Marketing Impacts the Role of Women in Entrepreneurship," just to name a couple.[19]

The network's leaders acknowledge that the expectations are high, though they do not simply leave students to flounder. BASIS recruits top-notch teachers, many from private industry, and these subject-matter experts tutor and work with students to actualize their full potential. Notably, BASIS teachers are not unionized and are rewarded for performance with bonuses.[20]

Erin Paradis, a school leader at BASIS, emphasized that with high expectations comes a lot of student support. "We know that we are expecting them to achieve at a very high level in their academics," Paradis stated, "so with that they need to have a balance in their life."[21] Students meet one-on-one each week with an academic support coach who helps them with organizational skills, test preparation, and time management. Critics say that the high expectations are unreasonable and lead to high attrition rates.[22] We say this is an indication that schooling is an intensely personal decision, and students and parents are constantly seeking to find the appropriate fit. We should not demonize schools holding students to high expectations simply because some students do not wish to pursue that level of rigor.

Reading about BASIS prompted some reflection on my own high school experience. My suburban public high school offered a number of AP courses, though you could not take them early; only one (AP World History) was offered in tenth grade, with the rest in eleventh or twelfth. As a dedicated athlete and a member of the newspaper staff in high school, I'm not entirely sure if I would have wanted to take many more of AP tests. That said, I recall feeling remarkably unchallenged in ninth and tenth grade, so probably I would have benefited from BASIS's accelerated curriculum. In twelfth grade, I would have loved the capstone project; I had almost no real-world learning in high school.

It is important to pause here to take stock of these achievements. Left largely to their own innovative devices, some charter schools have surmounted the two biggest and most urgent challenges facing American education: the racial academic gap and the international performance gap. We absolutely must learn from the distinctive traits that have made such successes possible and structure our education system to generate many more such successes.

What would happen if charter schools were not merely an occasional option but the principal means of delivering public education? At this we do not have to guess, because after Hurricane Katrina, New Orleans reorganized its horrifically failing school system into an all-charter system.

Now nearly two decades into the experiment, the transformation, according to the *Arizona Republic*, "has produced dramatic academic improvements in a district where the median household income is less than two-thirds the national average." The system is fueled by both public and private investments, which have produced new facilities and raised teacher salaries. (As we argued in the last chapter, similar increased funding could be accomplished by eliminating or downsizing school districts.) Roughly two-thirds of the schools are run by charter school management organizations, like InspireNOLA, which manages seven charter schools and has dramatically improved academic performance. The remaining schools are individually operated.[23]

Overall, the results are very impressive. Between 2004 and 2018, the high school graduation rate increased from 54 percent to 78 percent, the college entry rate rose from 37 to 60 percent, the share of New Orleans students attending the state's lowest-performing schools dropped from 62 to 8 percent, and the number of students attending A- or B-rated schools more than doubled. Patrick Dobard, chief executive of New Schools for New Orleans, remarked, "We had a totally broken system. The gains we have made are phenomenal."[24]

Most of the schools are open enrollment and use a lottery if demand exceeds supply. Schools receive higher funding for students whose native language is not English and for special-needs students. Charter schools in New Orleans cannot be operated by for-profit firms.[25]

The charter schools are responsible to the school district, but the district has far less control than before. The district monitors the schools' finances and academic performance. It intervenes if a school receives an F grade and can close a school if it receives a failing grade two years in a row. District staffers visit the schools to ensure compliance with special-education requirements and to make sure they are not inflating attendance. Otherwise, schools make their own personnel and budget decisions and can design and deliver their academic programs as they see fit.

New Orleans provides a transformational model for educational success. Although we propose autonomous community public schools, some states or school districts may opt for all-charter systems like New Orleans. At the same time, the role of the school district is dramatically transformed, from a political body that regulates nearly everything that goes on in the schools into an oversight role in which it monitors academic performance, financial accountability, and regulatory compliance. Basic governance, including the freedom to create distinctive educational programs, is devolved to the schools themselves. This deregulated, decentralized system can operate equally well whether the schools are charters operated by nonprofit organizations or state-sponsored autonomous public schools.

New Orleans is instructive for another reason: the city's educational shift proves that it literally took a natural disaster to unshackle the school system. What our nation has experienced with COVID-19 may provide a similar sudden, exogenous shock to the system that opens the door to meaningful long-term change.

Overcoming Opposition

Historically, charter schools have transcended the partisan divide. Indeed, they were initially proposed by American Federation of Teachers leader Albert Shanker.[26] Presidents Bill Clinton and Barack Obama were strong supporters of charter schools. Many liberal families send their children to charter schools, and based on racial and income demographics, the traditional constituencies of Democratic politicians send their children to charter schools as well.

But lately charter schools have become casualties of increased partisan stridency, especially as they have been championed by President Donald Trump and Education Secretary Betsy DeVos. As recently as 2010, there was little difference in support for charter schools among Democrats and Republicans. Yet by 2018, 75 percent of Republicans supported charter schools, while support among Democrats fell to 45 percent. Overall, support for charters fell from 65 percent in 2016 to an all-time low of 52 percent in 2017. But by 2018, support had rebounded to 62 percent, due entirely to increased support from

Republicans, with no change among Democrats. Still, support was especially strong for charter schools from two major Democratic constituencies, African Americans and Hispanics.[27]

Echoing powerful teachers' unions, which play a central role in party politics, most of the 2020 Democratic candidates for president took hostile positions toward charter schools. Their positions led Black and Hispanic charter school parents to protest at campaign events.[28] Those protests reflected overwhelming support for charter schools among Democratic primary voters, especially African Americans.[29]

Senator Cory Booker (D-NJ), who was among the Democratic presidential candidates, had a different take. As mayor of Newark, he presided over systemic public school reform and the growth of charter schools, which greatly expanded opportunities and improved academic performance in the impoverished city, in which 79 percent of the students qualify for free and reduced lunch. The charter schools helped boost the city's graduation rate over eight years from 61 to 76 percent. By 2015, Newark's charter schools were among the best in the nation, with 60 percent of their students scoring proficient in English versus 35 percent in traditional public schools, and 48 percent scoring proficient in math as compared to 26 percent of their public school counterparts. North Star Academy Charter School, whose students are 98 percent nonwhite and 85 percent poor, is one of the state's top-ranked public high schools.[30]

Drawing upon this experience, Senator Booker criticized his fellow Democratic presidential candidates for opposing charter schools. "The treatment by many Democratic politicians of high-performing public charter schools as boogeymen has undermined the fact that many of these schools are serving low-income urban children across the country in ways that are inclusive, equitable, publicly accountable and locally driven." He touted the success of charter schools as a cornerstone of his public education reforms, boosting the city's graduation rate from 50 percent to 77 percent and leading the nation in the number of beat-the-odds, high-performing schools. "The promise of better schools someday down the road," Booker urged, "doesn't do much for children who have to go to schools that fail them today."[31]

The major driver of charter school opposition is teachers' unions, for a simple reason: most charter schools are not unionized. The schools usually prefer not to have a collective-bargaining agreement in order to maintain control over salaries and other personnel decisions. Many charter schools consider such flexibility essential to their success, enabling them to pay more to teach subjects with low teacher supply, hire noncertified teachers, provide performance-based bonuses and raises, and fire poorly performing teachers. But charter schools and unions (in their local rather than national form) are not necessarily mutually exclusive.[32] Yet, in practice, unions have largely viewed charter schools as competitors to be destroyed at all costs.

Nationwide, only about 12 percent of charter schools are unionized. Of those, almost one-third are "conversion" schools—schools that converted from district schools to charter schools. Several states require charter conversion schools to retain the districts' collective-bargaining agreements.[33] Moving from district schools to state-sponsored community schools could have this same feature: if the school was unionized prior to its conversion, the collective-bargaining agreement would follow the transition. As always, teachers can decertify a union if they deem it unnecessary, and that could happen frequently in schools where teachers play a central role in governance. Indeed, Rebecca Friedrichs, a public school teacher for twenty-eight years, charges that teachers' unions are more focused on national politics than local teacher representation. She now works to empower teachers to form local associations that reflect their interests.[34] Teachers will continue to have a choice either way.

But for now, teachers' unions are growing more militant in their opposition to charter schools. Unions are no longer merely promoting their members' interests and stifling new reforms—they are now using their considerable muscle to roll back reforms that have improved education and expanded student opportunities. *The Economist* sagely summarized the situation: "The problem is that the teacher unions are at their strongest in precisely the places where charters are best."[35] And often where they are most needed.

A 2019 teachers' union strike in the Los Angeles Unified School District targeted charter schools. Owing to the district's low test scores, roughly one in five students have fled to charter schools. The unions' response? Prevent new charter schools from opening, thereby preventing students from escaping a chronically failing school district. The gambit succeeded: as part of the strike settlement, the district agreed to ask the state to cap the number of charter schools.[36] Similarly, in West Virginia, a teacher strike resulted in killing the state's first charter school, which was to be a STEM school operated in collaboration with Marshall University and West Virginia University.[37]

The unions' rallying cry is fighting the "privatization" of public schools. The slogan resonates: many believe that having private enterprises operate public schools, even if they are nonprofit entities, will be the death knell for an institution they hold dear.

The fear is, at best, overblown. Surely there are instances in which charter school operators have used their schools as personal ATMs, and well-designed programs should safeguard against that. At the same time, some unscrupulous public school officials have abused their positions of public trust. We strongly support transparency and accountability for all users of taxpayer dollars; charter schools enjoy a certain inherent advantage in that regard, because they are judged by performance.

Regardless, we hope that our proposal will help alleviate privatization concerns. We envision state-sponsored community schools that enjoy all of the autonomy and other advantages of charter schools *while retaining their complete identity as public schools*. Charter schools are public schools contracted out to private (usually nonprofit) entities; community schools would be public schools operated as such in a deregulated, decentralized environment, governed by public boards and accountable directly to the state.

Subjecting public schools to political control and stifling regulation has not worked. That toxic combination arrests innovation and stifles the talents of teachers and administrators. Yet that is the dominant form of governance for the vast majority of public schools. We need to make a clean break from the past: *all* public schools should be largely self-governing, held accountable, and rewarded for success. Indeed, even in our current highly regulated structure, some public schools thrive due to strong leadership and exceptional teachers. The state should reward such efforts, even as it carefully monitors and intervenes in failing schools.

How should we measure success? We should not assume that high test scores are necessarily correlated with the best schools. Instead, our focus should be on academic growth.

Analyzing data from Stanford University's Educational Opportunity Project, Dr. Matthew Ladner divided schools into four quadrants based on academic proficiency and growth. Many schools have high proficiency and low growth, meaning that although their students perform well on standardized tests, the schools are not meaningfully moving them along in terms of academic growth. The best schools have both high academic proficiency and high growth; the worst (which demand the greatest intervention) combine low academic proficiency and low growth. The most hopeful sign is schools that are low on academic proficiency but high on growth, because if their trajectory persists, the schools will become top performers. Dr. Ladner identifies two high-poverty Arizona charter schools, Reyes Maria Ruiz Leadership Academy in south Phoenix and Mexicayotl Academy in Nogales, at the Mexican border, as low-proficiency schools that have some of the greatest growth in the nation. That type of success should be supported and replicated. As Dr. Ladner observes, efforts "to micromanage a sprawling field of schools generally end in frustration, but policymakers on their A-games can provide incentives and resources to help educators achieve and sustain success."[38]

Reform efforts should be directed toward unshackling schools along the lines that have generated charter school success. Schools should be largely self-governing, allowed to develop distinctive educational programs, to prioritize resources, and to reward outstanding teachers. They should be open to all, transparent, financially accountable, and held responsible for results. But they should be allowed to succeed or fail, and to make the essential decisions necessary for success.

All advocates for high-quality educational opportunities should champion charter schools and other options. At the same time, we must recognize that the vast majority of children attend traditional public schools. Instead of destroying promising options like charter schools, we should learn from what makes them successful and extend the same autonomy to traditional public schools. In a word, what the public schools need is what has made America the greatest engine of opportunity in the history of the world: freedom.

CHAPTER 5

Hiring and Retaining Great Teachers— and Paying Them (Much) More

The centerpiece of any successful educational enterprise is great teachers.

We all remember teachers who taught us well and inspired us, who invested boundless energy in their students and left us all wanting more. We also all remember teachers who were ill suited to the classroom, either by temperament or deficient skills, or who were burned out long before we entered their classrooms.

In most public schools, both types of teachers are paid exactly the same. Every time we increase teacher salaries across the board, we give raises to the best teachers—and to the worst. The best teachers could make much more money doing something else, and we often lose them because they are underpaid and stifled by bureaucracy. They are prohibited by law from negotiating salaries, conditions, or bonuses that would keep them motivated and working as teachers. The worst teachers are permanently protected in their jobs by tenure laws and are incentivized to remain in their positions as long as necessary to collect lifetime retirement and healthcare benefits.

To fix our K–12 education system, it is absolutely essential to fix our teacher compensation system.

We must attract the best and the brightest to the teaching ranks. We must treat them as the prized professionals they are. We need to remove barriers to hiring the best, firing the worst, and compensating teachers according to their demonstrated skills and accomplishments.

Now is a perfect time to do that. The teaching profession will change greatly in the coming decades. In recent years, we have experienced a classroom teacher shortage. But as the nature of teaching evolves, we may need fewer teachers standing in front of classrooms in coming years. As technology advances, we can put the best teachers in front of vastly more students.

Computers will play a much greater role in individualized learning, even in the classroom context. In both situations, classroom teachers will monitor individual progress and provide focused support. We will need many more teachers to create online academic content.

As we witnessed during the COVID-19 pandemic, when we moved to nearly an entire nation of students engaged in distance-based learning, some schools and teachers were able to adapt effectively to the dramatically changed educational landscape and others were not. States such as Florida provided students with devices so that teachers could regularly check in and monitor their progress, while districts in South Carolina, Indiana, and Illinois repurposed school buses as WiFi hot spots to ensure students had access to the web.[1] These innovative responses stand in stark contrast to districts that—more than a month after they closed their doors—had not provided any instruction and were barely reviewing or grading work at all.[2] Teachers' unions pushed for the latter practice.[3] The virus gave us a preview of how we may deliver much of our education in the future and what skills are most valuable to take advantage of the new tools at our disposal.

Unshackling Teacher Recruitment, Training, and Compensation

Teacher recruitment and compensation distinguish the United States from other industrialized countries that provide a higher-quality education to their students. As OECD's Andreas Schleicher observes, "Nowhere does the quality of a school system exceed the quality of its teachers."[4] More successful countries place a priority on recruitment and development of highly qualified teachers. In Singapore, teachers are recruited from the top third of secondary school graduates, and only one-fifth of those who apply are admitted to teacher training; in Finland, a smaller percentage of applicants is accepted into teacher training than to law school.[5] In grim contrast, in the United States, students majoring in education ranked twenty-sixth out of thirty-eight majors on the Scholastic Aptitude Test.[6]

The vast majority of American schoolteachers are products of university schools of education and certified by the state. As both authors can attest, having gone through the specified training and earned teacher certification, although education classes can be valuable (especially for specialized education, such as for working with children with disabilities), every moment spent in a prescribed education class is a moment away from classes that build subject-matter proficiency. And the pool of certified teachers is finite, artificially limiting the pool of potential teachers.

Many charter schools rarely hire certified teachers, especially for high school, and instead recruit college graduates who excelled in their majors or hire from professional ranks (including scientists, mathematicians, and linguists). Likewise, nontraditional teacher preparation programs such as Teach for America (TFA) and the Alliance for Catholic Education (ACE) recruit highly qualified college graduates to teach in economically challenged schools. TFA provides its own teacher-training program and has placed more than sixty thousand graduates in public schools across the United States. Even though their backgrounds and training are unconventional, TFA teachers have produced stellar academic results.[7] Many TFA alumni have gone on to lead schools or create their own. Similarly, ACE places teachers in underserved Catholic schools across the country, reaching one of four Catholic schools nationwide, and offers a rigorous school leadership preparation program.[8]

Rigid teacher certification requirements create a barrier to highly qualified individuals entering the teacher workforce. We should seek to attract the best and the brightest, whether they have formal teacher credentials or not.

Recruiting and retaining highly qualified teachers means compensating them as highly qualified professionals. We actually do a better job of that than most people realize or are led to believe. Although two-thirds of Americans believe teachers are underpaid, the general public also thinks teachers make about $18,000 less than their actual average salary.[9] Overall, the United States ranks seventh in teacher pay among industrialized nations, with an average salary topping out at $71,000 for high school and $67,000 for elementary school.[10]

But we could do much better, especially if we reduced the massive bureaucracy surrounding education. The impact of administrative growth and bloat on teacher salaries is stark: even as US educational expenditures between 1992 and 2014 were rising substantially and school districts were hiring more administrators and support staff, the average teacher salary nationwide was *reduced* by 2 percent.[11] If we apply the prescriptions of the prior chapters—even a little bit!—we will free up significant education dollars to spend on academics, which translates into higher teacher salaries.

Mortgaging Our Future

Another massive obstacle to improved teacher compensation is a hidden behemoth that must be discussed openly and confronted vigorously: teacher pension liabilities. These pension obligations compensate for past employment and do not contribute at all to current educational performance—yet they divert enormous and growing resources from current educational needs.

Most public school teachers are contractually entitled to lifetime pensions and generous health benefits following a modest number of years of service. Like many public pensions, teacher pension systems are often underfunded because the teacher and taxpayer contributions are inadequate to fund promised benefits. The combined effect of generous and underfunded pension benefits is that *an ever-growing share of school district budgets is devoted to people who no longer contribute to the educational enterprise.* In California, for instance, voters in 2012 approved a 30 percent tax increase to fund schools—yet all of the extra revenue was diverted to pensions and healthcare costs for retired teachers to keep the system afloat.[12]

This conundrum is painfully illustrated by the massive Los Angeles Unified School District (LAUSD). Between 2001 and 2019, LAUSD increased spending by 55.5 percent. Yet salaries increased by only 24.4 percent, less than half that amount, and the share of the overall budget devoted to instructional salaries shrank from 44.4 to 33.5 percent. Employee benefits, however, soared by 138.2 percent. When a district promises free medical, dental, and vision coverage to all retired employees and their spouses after only five years of service, it must find this money somewhere. These benefits alone cost $314 million in 2019, yet obviously generated no classroom benefits.[13] Indeed, they detract from the educational enterprise, because they mean fewer resources for classrooms and teacher salaries.

Similarly, in the Chicago Public Schools, the pension system is only 51.5 percent funded and is $9 billion in debt. Contributing only 2 percent of their salaries, career teachers receive an average annual pension of $73,350 and over $2 million in aggregate lifetime benefits—more than police or fire-fighters. Chicago has more retired teachers receiving benefits than active ones paying into the system.[14] The escalating pension costs will consume an ever-larger share of public school expenditures. Statewide, the top two hundred Illinois public school pension beneficiaries, mostly retired administrators, are collecting from $160,000 to over $300,000 per year in pension benefits.

The *Arizona Republic* recently warned that the state's 20 percent across-the-board teacher salary increase could be consumed by increased pension contributions. As the newspaper notes, required teacher contributions have quadrupled to 12 percent of salary since 2002, "which dips into take-home pay and ties up taxpayer funds that could be used elsewhere, like giving teach-ers additional pay raises."[15] Stock market losses during the pandemic could place underfunded teacher pension funds on even shakier financial footing, requiring an even greater allocation of the resources earmarked for education.

A private-sector firm would likely plunge into bankruptcy under the bur-den of such pension liabilities. Public school teachers are exempt from Social Security (freeing a significant portion of their salaries for other investments), so some provision must be made for retirement. But generous defined-benefit pensions, without employee and employer contributions sufficient to make them financially sound, are unsustainable. Worse, they result in an ever-growing diversion of current resources away from the classroom. Public schools must either provide less generous retirement benefits or face the pros-pect of continued increased taxpayer expenditures devoted not to salaries or other classroom expenditures but to rising costs for paying those who are no longer in the system.

Charter schools rarely provide defined-benefit pensions, instead allocat-ing as much as possible for current compensation, including retirement fund contributions. If we were starting afresh, other public schools would do well to follow their example. But the law protects existing beneficiaries and pen-sion investments. Schools should change the system for new teachers, either providing them with defined-contribution retirement plans, reducing pension benefits, or increasing employee contributions. Otherwise, we will continue to mortgage our children's future while limiting our ability to attractively compensate excellent teachers.

Rewarding Great Teachers

Freeing resources for greater teacher compensation should not mean across-the-board salary increases, which equally reward the best and the worst. As Kate Walsh, president of the National Council on Teacher Quality, puts it, tying pay to seniority and education levels rather than performance "allows us to set up this facade where we pretend that all teachers are equally gifted and bring equal skills to the table."[16] As anyone reading this book can attest, not all teachers are alike in their ability to teach. We should concentrate resources on recruiting and retaining our best teachers.

We also need to differentiate salaries so that teachers in hard-to-staff subjects—whether math, science, Mandarin, or others where teachers are in short supply—are attracted to the teaching profession. That does not mean they are worth more; they are just much scarcer, and schools are competing for their talents.

At the same time, teachers in all subjects should be eligible for bonuses if they add demonstrable value to their students' academic growth. We should measure that added value based on where the students start. Advanced students may be far ahead of their grade level before the academic year even starts; their teachers should be rewarded not for past achievements but only for additional growth. The same goes for teachers whose students are academically behind: bringing those students closer to grade level merits financial reward.

Teacher performance measures should not reflect test scores alone. Recent research indicates that teachers can also exert measurable influence on non-cognitive skills such as adaptability, motivation, and self-discipline, which Northwestern University professor C. Kirabo Jackson notes are "key determinants of adult outcomes."[17] Indeed, Professor Jackson finds that a student's behavior index is a much stronger predictor of success than test scores.[18] Although teachers who help produce higher test scores also tend to improve behavior, the two measures are different.[19] Thus, he concludes, "the lion's share of truly excellent teachers—-those who improve long-run outcomes—will not be identified using test-score value added alone."[20]

This research suggests that teacher performance should be measured by a range of objective criteria. But it should be measured, with good teachers being rewarded and bad teachers being remediated or shown the door.

This is all a far cry from the status quo, where teachers in most districts are paid the same as others with similar credentials, regardless of whether they are successful. By contrast, charter schools often pay teachers differently based on the skills they bring and the results they produce. (The teaching market is vastly freer and more competitive in postsecondary education as well.) As a result, despite typically lower per-pupil funding, teachers in charter schools can sometimes reach six-figure salaries. That should be much, much more common for our best teachers.

Roadblocks to Reform

Why is skill-, merit-, and result-based pay the exception rather than the rule in K–12 education?

The answer is simple: most school districts are unionized, and predominant union practice is to negotiate collective-bargaining agreements that dictate salaries based primarily on seniority rather than skills, merit, and results. The OECD's Schleicher remarks that "the American style of union-management relations . . . may have produced a more rule-bound environment than is found in systems embracing more professional forms of work organisation."[21] As University of Chicago law professor Omri Ben-Shahar remarks, salary increases "go to both good teachers and bad, giving bad teachers as much incentive as good ones to become and remain teachers."[22] At the same time, it is illegal in most instances to reward teachers based on outstanding performance.

Unions also negotiate tenure rules that make it very difficult to fire teachers based on performance. Thus, as University of Arkansas professor Jay Greene observes, "Despite years of 'high-stakes' student testing, very few of the nation's

3.14 million public-school teachers have ever lost a job, had their pay reduced, or otherwise faced meaningful consequences because of these test results."[23]

By doing these things, unions are doing exactly what they exist for: to represent their members' interests, which they are legally obligated to do even if those interests are inconsistent with the educational mission.[24] But the one-size-fits-all system that results from collective bargaining makes it very difficult to reward and incentivize excellence and to penalize failure. While respecting the right of teachers to organize as well as the benefits the unions can bring to their members, we have to figure out ways to make the system work better for its intended beneficiaries—the students—by making it easier to hire and retain great teachers, reward the best, and get rid of the worst.

Ideally, unions and reformers would work in tandem to improve our nation's education system. All advanced societies revere teachers and recognize their critical role in any education system. But the organizations that represent teachers are often the most powerful and intransigent opponents of essential reforms, because they incorrectly perceive (and loudly proclaim) that such reforms are harmful to teachers. That is not true, because educational excellence requires rewarding our best teachers.

Many of our nation's leading education reformers, both liberal and conservative, have come to recognize how difficult it is to achieve meaningful reforms in the face of union opposition. Joel Klein, who brought valuable experience as head of the US Justice Department's Antitrust Division under President Bill Clinton to his position as chancellor of the New York City Public Schools for eight years under Mayor Michael Bloomberg, explained how unions thwarted needed reforms in the nation's largest public school system. Among many other reforms, Klein proposed using value-added measures to determine teacher tenure. The union responded by successfully pushing a state law to block the use of test data in tenure decisions. "As a result," says Klein, "even when making a lifetime tenure commitment, under New York law you could not consider a teacher's impact on student learning. That Kafkaesque outcome demonstrates precisely the way the system is run: for the adults."[25]

Klein reports that New York City pays $100 million every year for teachers who don't teach because of incompetence or malfeasance but can't be fired. He notes that because of collective bargaining, physical education teachers are paid the same as math teachers, despite the fact that highly qualified math teachers are in far greater demand. Seniority rules mean that the most experienced teachers can choose to work in safer, more affluent schools. Pay increases are automatic and unrelated to performance. And teacher pension funds face a $1 trillion shortfall, forcing the system to take money "from current and future operating budgets, robbing today's children to pay tomorrow's pensions."[26]

Klein proposes allowing teachers to opt out of defined-benefit pensions in return for higher salaries; increasing the use of technology; and hiring fewer, more highly qualified teachers and paying them more—all ideas we support. "If, going forward, we eliminated all of the automatic raises and promises of huge lifetime benefits," Klein argues, "we'd have an enormous amount of money to devote to merit pay, hardship-assignment incentives, and recruiting in subjects where we have shortages."[27] But the unions opposed all of those efforts.

Overcoming Obstacles

How can reform advocates possibly hope to overcome such strong resistance? As Joel Klein observes, "The forces behind reform seem scattered and weak," while "those defending the status quo . . . are well organized and well financed." Klein warns that "without a major realignment of political forces, we won't get the dramatic improvements our children need."[28]

As with any immovable object, the best strategy is to go around it. Reform advocates need to speak to, engage with, and enlist teachers—to call upon the worthy aspirations that motivated them to pursue their noble profession, to find common cause on every possible issue of mutual concern, and even to appeal to their self-interest. Surely most teachers—certainly all good teachers—believe they should be paid commensurately with their skills. And no teacher likes being subject to unnecessary bureaucracy.

As a result of a recent US Supreme Court decision, individual teachers will have greater autonomy to speak for themselves on public-policy issues. In *Janus v. American Federation of State, County, and Municipal Employees*, the court held that public employees who are not members of unions cannot be forced to pay "agency fees" to support union activities.[29] The court reasoned that it would violate the freedom of speech rights of nonmembers to force them to subsidize union activities and positions on matters of public importance with which they disagreed. A majority of the public, along with an equal majority of schoolteachers, agree that teachers should not be forced to pay agency fees if they are not union members.[30] The ruling could encourage some teachers to opt out of their unions if they disagree with their political and lobbying positions.

We hope that teachers and even their unions can support many of the reform proposals we are proposing. We have called for eliminating unnecessary bureaucracy and ending diversion of resources away from the classroom. As a reminder from earlier in the book, had we limited the growth of nonteaching personnel to student growth between 1992 and 2014, American public schools would have saved $35 billion per year—enough to give every teacher an $11,000 pay raise.[31] Imagine the savings if we actually eliminated much of the middleman bloat. To put it mildly, neither teachers nor their unions share identical interests with school districts. To the extent that reducing bureaucracy means giving more autonomy and control over how resources are spent to schools, principals, and teachers, reformers should be able to make common cause with teachers and their advocacy groups.

In the next chapter, we call for greater options for families, but teachers should have greater options as well. Instead of assigning teachers based on seniority, schools should be able to compete for the best teachers and to pay them accordingly. The best teachers should be able to earn in the six figures. But that prospect depends on greater flexibility, both for employers and employees, including the ability of individual teachers to shed their collective-bargaining straitjackets. Policy makers who are inclined to increase education spending should negotiate terms that help children, such as pay for performance.

The Dallas Independent School District recently eliminated seniority-based pay in favor of performance pay, with some teachers now making $80,000 to $90,000 per year. Star teachers who agree to teach in high-needs schools receive $8,000 to $10,000 in extra salary. The district, 90 percent of whose students are low income, has boosted achievement across all grades and subjects by 13 percent. The superintendent, Michael Hinojosa, says, "The fact that I don't have to deal with a union contract gives us a big advantage in being nimble and creative."[32]

Indeed, the worst consequence of collective bargaining in the education context is the tendency to think of teachers as an undifferentiated mass rather than as millions of individuals who bring different skills to the table. Imagine if an excellent teacher could dramatically improve her salary not by awaiting the results of a union negotiation process or by marching at the state capitol, but instead merely by teaching effectively and receiving an automatic bonus for doing exactly that. The vast majority of public school teachers cannot control their destinies in that way—except in charter schools, which as a result are often able to attract highly talented teachers even while receiving fewer public resources.

We may be able to move in that direction by offering existing teachers a choice: remaining in the existing seniority-based compensation system or opting out—taking the risk of not having guaranteed job security but opening up the reward of greater compensation based on objective measures of success. New teachers would be hired into the latter system. Over time, teachers could earn much higher salaries, and schools could retain and reward the best teachers.

The best teachers could also earn bonuses for teaching more students. The system has largely embraced smaller class sizes, which create greater costs but do not produce commensurate academic gains. We can turn that equation around: more students should have access to the best teachers, and the best teachers should be allowed (if they choose) to teach more students, with a bonus attached for doing so. Indeed, we can harness technology to provide virtual access to the best teachers, who can moonlight by taking their skills to video and the internet and increase their compensation by doing so.

For these dynamic innovations to occur—for these rewards to flow to highly skilled teachers—requires flexibility. Unfortunately, our K–12 school system is one of the least flexible in the world. All the more reason to devolve crucial decision making to the school level.

People respond to incentives. Systems do too. If we expect excellence, we need to reward excellence. We are so far removed from a system that rewards excellence, holds people accountable for performance, and allows resources to flow to their most effective use that the entire idea of creating such a system may seem impossible, especially given the powerful institutional resistance to change. But if those of us who truly put America's children's needs first align behind the reforms necessary to effectuate needed change —like hiring and rewarding great teachers—that force may prove irresistible.

CHAPTER 6

Toward an Unshackled System

In 1962, Milton Friedman wrote, "Not all schooling is education nor all education, schooling. The proper subject of concern is education."[1] If what we are really concerned about is education, providing funding through school districts is the last thing we should do. Instead, money should be transported to schools and educational services by students.

School choice policies enable this shift. These programs take as their maxim that all parents should be empowered to choose where, when, and how their child is educated. School choice—contrary to the widespread media narratives—comes in a variety of forms, including vouchers, tax-credit scholarships, and education savings accounts. After describing each policy in its own right, we conclude by arguing that education savings accounts provide parents and students with the most flexibility to obtain a twenty-first-century education.

Choice

Tying education to one's zip code is at best illogical and at worst stifling and marginalizing. The reality is that everyone has school choice in America except for the poor. Why did you choose to move to your neighborhood? If you have children, odds are it had something to do with the local schools. In fact, the most common moment for Americans to move out of cities and into the suburbs is when they start families. Certain cities have hemorrhaged residents over the past decade and report a net decline in population even with new births taken into account.[2] Though parents report various reasons for leaving, they know that neighborhoods have a great effect on future outcomes. Indeed, research finds your zip code is predictive of later-in-life outcomes even when controlling for all other factors.[3] In modern America, those who reside in your neighborhood are also enrolled in your school. The structural inequalities of your neighborhood, such as run-down facilities, type of grocery stores, or lack of health facilities, are also reflected by your school. If you are poor, you are trapped—unable to move to a different district or afford private school.

Choice as it currently functions is a piecemeal endeavor. Some states have vouchers, some have scholarships for low-income students funded through tax credits, some have education savings accounts (ESAs). This array of mechanisms is confusing even to astute observers. Though we do not deny the political realities of education reform, states that want to increase educational and economic opportunity should adopt choice and a simplified funding formula for education. Current funding formulas are an absolute mess in most states. As previously discussed, the amount of money poured into a district has an almost inverse relationship with its output of educated young adults. Moreover, even if a newly elected governor perceives waste or wants a more efficient allocation of funds, powerful opponents (unions and special-interest groups) will immediately label that person as a leader who wants to "slash education funding" or "privatize education." These labels are unfair, but it is obvious why someone concerned about politics would want to avoid them.

We propose that funding should be given to all parents or families at a base level. Since we have no idea how much it actually takes to educate students, this number could be somewhere around the average state per-pupil funding amount. These numbers already vary widely among the states. Additional funding should be provided to certain families, such as those who are poor or have children with disabilities, through a sliding scale based on need. Regardless of the per-pupil number, funding must be equalized across sectors. Currently, voucher and tax-credit scholarship programs in several states are unable to compete with charter schools due to lesser funding. Though it sounds pretty good if a state offers a voucher for $5,000, if private school tuition costs $8,000, the family is left to cover the extra $3,000 or not attend (although many private schools are able to make their scholarship offerings go further when low-income students bring vouchers). That same child can attend a charter school free, however, because she takes with her the equivalent of per-pupil spending at her prior public school. A charter school is therefore a more financially viable option compared to attending a private school using a voucher.

Once funding has been allocated on an equitable basis, a system should exist through which parents can learn about their options. Rather than being told that their child is expected to attend Public School 65 on September 1, parents should be able to investigate all available schooling options. It could be as easy as picking a movie on Netflix. The education system of the future should allow parents to log on to a single platform to view information about local school offerings and to track records of success, parent testimonials, and other information. Presented with the various options in an aggregated format, parents are empowered to make an informed choice for their child, or at least narrow down their options.

Tennessee created a similar tool after passing an education savings account school choice policy in 2019. Its "compare" feature allows parents to select any school and compare it to others in an easily digestible table. Private and charter schools can even post links to their scholarship and financial aid applications for parents to easily access.[4] The nonprofit Choose a School website in Arizona provides similar information. The education sector will always have some information asymmetries—when one party in an exchange of services possesses more knowledge about the product than another—but simplifying the process for understanding the educational options that exist is long overdue.

Competition

To give families authentic choice, competition among educational providers must also exist. Competition is commonplace in midsize to large cities, where one can hardly walk a block without stumbling upon a different school. Though schools are not focused on profit maximization and students are not widgets, there is much to be said for competition disrupting the status quo in education. Before choice programs came into being, the traditional public school sector had relatively little competition for just under a century. Rather, it enjoyed a state-sponsored monopoly. Nothing was pushing these schools to get better, so many stagnated and did not change with the times. As we have already outlined, this especially affected urban areas, and students are still feeling the effects today.

Yet areas where choice programs entered into the equation have inspired improvement in the traditional public school sector. Of the thirty-three empirical studies on public schools in choice areas, thirty-one find that choice actually improves academic outcomes in public schools. Only two found neutral or negative effects.[5] The rules of economics are not suspended at the schoolhouse doors, and public schools, just like other service providers, respond to competition (and as we urged in the preceding chapters, they should possess far greater autonomy to do so).

A common refrain is that choice drains resources from public schools. Actually, it allows students who are not doing well in the system to exit, but it leaves many of the resources (including all local funding) in the schools. This means that even though the district no longer has the responsibility to educate that child, it still keeps a significant portion of that child's funds. Thus, rather than losing money, local public schools in areas of choice have more money to spend on fewer students.[6] Despite this fact, it's challenging for researchers to isolate *what* exactly is causing public schools in areas with choice to improve. Yet it's clear that their improvement coincided with the onset of parental choice programs.

 Former Milwaukee Public Schools superintendent Dr. Howard Fuller, founder of the Black Alliance for Educational Options, supported the voucher program there because it gave him leverage to improve the public schools. Reform opponents predicted disaster, but Milwaukee has a plethora of public and private educational options today, many of them thriving.

Though competition is clearly present in urban areas, school choice policies that enable home or virtual schooling bring competition to rural areas too. Large public school districts are typically the largest employer in rural districts.[7] It is very difficult for private or charter schools to compete in these markets, especially if the supply of teachers or facilities is lacking. Thus, the best way to harness the power of competition in rural districts is through education savings accounts. As we will discuss later, ESAs allow families to use their education funds for a wide variety of services and materials. For rural districts that lack brick-and-mortar alternatives to district public schools, ESAs can aid families preferring to homeschool, hire tutors, or access virtual education. Though the driver of competition has been historically nonexistent in rural districts, it is now made possible with the internet and an ESA policy.

A great way for states to increase competition is to reduce barriers to entry for educational providers. The process for chartering a school is overregulated in some states, as unions and antichoice advocates have lobbied for caps on charter schools and provisions that impose waiting periods and hefty paperwork for charter management organizations.[8] Though accountability is important, regulations such as these might prevent schools with innovative models from opening.[9] The true accountability should be between families and schools; if a school opens and there is no demand for it, it will not be able to sustain itself on a year-to-year basis. State policies should enable and incentivize different models; our system should be as diverse as the students in our nation. Competition will only be possible if distinct modes of schooling exist.

Cutting through the Media Noise

The media has perpetuated a series of myths and misconceptions about school choice for years. Their faulty narratives and cherry-picked statistics present a significant impediment to education reform. Ensuring that choice and competition become a reality requires rebutting the most powerful narratives against their existence. Here are the most pervasive myths:

Myth: School choice harms public schools.

The first, and most common, argument levied against school choice programs is that they harm the traditional public school sector. Critics are primarily concerned about (1) harm to public schools generally and (2) the loss of funding specifically.

Most research finds that choice helps improve public schools. A study by Northwestern University researchers found that public school students living in areas with more private school options saw test score gains at higher rates than those living in areas with fewer private school options.[10] These findings echo those of thirty-one out of thirty-three other nationwide empirical studies, which show improved academic outcomes for students who remain in public schools after choice programs are implemented.[11] Similarly, a recent statewide study of Florida's academic achievement concluded that outcomes for public school students improved as the Florida Tax Credit Scholarship expanded. Lower-income students benefit the most; those attending the public schools most subject to competition from private schools witnessed gains in test scores and reductions in rates of absenteeism and suspension.[12] If school choice on balance were really a threat, as critics allege, why has Florida's public school sector (and those of other states) improved after these programs were introduced?

As we discussed in prior chapters, very little correlation exists between the amount of education spending and student achievement. Regardless, as a normative matter, do mechanisms of choice divert funds from district public schools? The answer: it depends. States fund public education in myriad ways.[13] Many, such as Florida, tie funding to the number of students in the public school system rather than the number of teachers or classrooms.[14] Yet when students switch from a district public school to private school using a scholarship or to a charter school, it provides a net financial benefit to the state.

Though tax credits impose a fiscal cost to governments by reducing the amount of tax revenues received, they also produce a benefit to state and local governments when students choose to leave or not enroll in public schools. The schools to which these students—called "switchers"—move are educating more efficiently, spending less money per student but producing greater gains. A study of the Florida Tax Credit Scholarship's fiscal impact found that the program had saved taxpayers between $372 and $550 million since its inception. For the program to be fiscally neutral, 74–81 percent of scholarship students must choose to leave or not attend public schools.[15] For the program to do actual fiscal harm, over 81 percent of students must leave public schools.

Thus, the amount of taxpayer funds required to educate children in public schools is reduced when those schools have fewer students. As EdChoice's Martin Lueken writes, "A potential by-product of school choice programs is that they result in more resources for each student remaining in a public school. . . . Thus, while it may be the case that total revenue for a given public school may drop, it is usually not the case that revenue per student declines."[16] States may then choose to direct these savings to public schools or other public services.

Myth: Schools of choice cherry-pick students.

Another common media critique of choice programs and charter schools is that they "cherry-pick" or "cream-skim" either the strongest academic students or the relatively more advantaged students, leaving behind the most disadvantaged (academically or financially) in public schools.

Yet the evidence shows that schools of choice serve the students who are *more* disadvantaged, both academically and socioeconomically, than their district public school peers. Nationwide, the makeup of charter schools includes 33 percent Hispanic students and 26 percent Black students—more than the traditional public school serves in either demographic.[17] More than 75 percent of students are eligible for free or reduced-price lunch at 33 percent of charter schools versus 24 percent of public schools.[18] Moreover, nearly all charter schools enroll via lottery, because student demand far eclipses the number of available seats. By definition, lottery is a form of random assignment. Similarly, private school choice programs that provide vouchers for low-income students serve overwhelmingly Black and Hispanic student populations. The argument that choice schools cherry-pick the best students is just wrong.

Myth: Schools of choice have less oversight.

Another erroneous claim against schools of choice is that they have less oversight than their district public school counterparts. This claim entirely misses the fact that schools of choice actually have dual accountability. They are responsive to both the state *and* parents, who are empowered to vote with their feet. Because parents chose the school in the first place, they can withdraw their children at any time. Online interfaces giving parents transparency into school successes and failures, such as those in Tennessee and Arizona referenced above, will also help. When parents are educated and empowered about their options and can vote with their feet, this increases accountability. As the Cato Institute's Andrew Coulson explains, market forces work to benefit even the relatively less informed parents: "Each school in a competitive market has to offer the most effective services it can, at the lowest possible cost, or risk losing the business of every family that takes the time to compare prices and outcomes. As a result, even parents who do not spend weeks or months in faithful comparison shopping benefit from the efforts of those who do."[19]

Myth: School choice increases segregation.

"Make no mistake: This use of privatization, coupled with disinvestment are only slightly more polite cousins of segregation," claimed American Federation of Teachers president Randi Weingarten about private school choice in a speech in 2017.[20] In reality, the exact opposite is true; indeed, it is the zoning system for traditional public schools that segregates.[21] As neighborhoods become more stratified by income, race, and class, so, too, do the schools they contain.[22] Suburban district schools look far different from their inner-city counterparts. School choice programs, on the other hand, help to *mitigate* the effects of residential segregation, providing low-income students of color an escape route to other schools.

Initial studies of the Ohio school choice program found that 70 percent of students in the city's public schools, as compared to less than 38 percent of voucher students, attended a school with 70 percent or greater minority enrollment. Similarly, in Milwaukee, the percentage of students attending a 90 percent minority school in the early years of the voucher program was 54.4 percent among public school students, 49.8 percent for all voucher students, and 41.8 percent for voucher students attending religious schools.[23] More recently, an aggregate 2019 review of private school choice programs found a small but positive integrative effect.[24]

Myth: School choice is synonymous with vouchers.

The mainstream media loves to call all school choice programs by the same name: "vouchers." They have succeeded in making this a politically unpopular term and now label all school choice policies with it. Vouchers, however, are only one species of school choice. There are many other policies putting education dollars and decision making into the hands of parents. We think details matter; school choice programs are really quite diverse and deserve to be understood as such. Figure 1 outlines a side-by-side comparison of their nuances.[25]

Education Savings Accounts (ESAs) as the Ideal Model

Although all types of school choice expand educational opportunities, the ultimate twenty-first-century policy is the education savings account (ESA). ESAs are the closest model for consumer-driven education funding. They enable parents to personally tailor the education of their children rather than merely choosing among school options (if they even get to do that). ESAs are the most effective way to promote choice and competition, which are key drivers of innovation and quality in nearly every facet of American life. They can be key drivers of innovation and quality in education as well.

These accounts are placed at the disposal of all eligible families, who can use them for any educational expense—not just private school tuition but distance learning, software, educational therapies, community college courses, extracurricular activities, and on and on. Schools receive their funding not through political processes but through consumer choice, making providers accountable and responsive to students. Unused funds can be saved for college or vocational training. ESAs support demand for new educational services.

Vouchers	Tax-Credit Scholarships
18 states + Washington, DC	18 states
192,660 students used a voucher in 2019.	289,260 students used a TCS in 2019.

Public Taxes	• Citizens pay income and sales taxes to the state.	Public Donations	• Individuals and corporations choose to donate money to the scholarship program, receiving a tax credit in return.
State	• The state collects taxes from citizens and decides on a per-pupil funding amount for the voucher.	Nonprofit	• A nonprofit scholarship granting organization (SGO) manages the donated money, distributing it to qualified applicants.
Parents	• Parents choose the school that is the best fit for the child, whether public or private.	Parents	• Parents choose the school that is the best fit for their child, whether public or private.
School	• Participating schools accept students with vouchers, allowing that money to cover all or part of their tuition.	School	• Participating schools accept students with tax-credit scholarships, allowing that money to cover all or part of their tuition.

FIGURE 1. Comparison of school choice programs. *Source:* Kate J. Hardiman

No one knows the real cost to educate a child, yet we continue to increase the dollar amount that we guesstimate it takes. ESAs, insofar as they encourage a prudent allocation of resources by consumers of education, move society closer to efficient provision of this good. Moreover, Brookings recently found that only 60 percent of rural families have access to schools of choice.[26] Thus, families in rural districts wanting a way out of district schooling are sometimes left out of the conversation. The marriage of education savings accounts and the student-centric technology we discuss in a later chapter has the power to give families living in even the most remote locations meaningful educational choice.

ation Savings Accounts

tes

9 students used ESAs in 2019.

1	Type 2

Type 1

- Public Taxes
  - Citizens pay income and sales taxes to the state.
- State
  - The state collects taxes from citizens and decides on a per-pupil funding amount for the ESA.
- Parents
  - Parents receive funds on a debit card.
- Educational Expenses
  - Parents pay for preapproved educational expenses such as tuition, tutors, and books with their ESA.
- Overseer
  - Parents provide receipts monthly or quarterly to a program overseer.

Type 2

- Public Donations
  - Citizens donate to a nonprofit.
- Nonprofit
  - The nonprofit distributes funds to parents.
- Parents
  - Parents receive funds on a debit card.
- Educational Expenses
  - Parents pay for preapproved educational expenses such as tuition, tutors, and books with their ESA.
- Overseer
  - Parents provide receipts monthly or quarterly to a program overseer.

Six states—Arizona, Florida, Mississippi, North Carolina, Nevada, and Tennessee—have adopted ESAs to varying degrees.[27] ESAs allow families to individualize their child's education. We believe they should replace the current byzantine and unequal education formulas and provide the means for *all* families to obtain the education that best serves their children's needs, including public schools. As we previously argued, having most funding go to schools through families rather than bureaucracies will transform education by empowering both families and the schools they choose.

Defenders of the status quo are striking back against ESAs through lawsuits and ballot measures, underscoring their systemic impact. ESAs transform the role of government from a monopoly education provider into a funder and enabler of individualized education services. Traditional public schools will continue to enjoy inherent advantages, such as state funding for infrastructure costs, but they will obtain their funding from consumers rather than government and thus will be incentivized to improve their quality and personalize their offerings to attract students.

An Introduction to ESAs

An ESA is a state- or third party–funded savings account earmarked for education. Parents can withdraw their children from their public district or charter school and receive a deposit of public funds into government-authorized savings accounts. They can then direct those funds toward any approved educational expense. The important advantage of an ESA is that the funds can cover any combination of services, allowing parents to truly treat education as a customizable commodity.[28] No longer will we have a one-size-fits-all system.

Funding mechanisms and qualification requirements for ESAs differ by state. Some programs specifically aid children with disabilities or low-income students, while others are available to all students attending a district public school. Variation also exists in whether ESAs are used for reimbursement of already purchased education expenses or for real-time purchasing.

In general, there are two ways to fund ESAs. The first uses public funds from state coffers (similar to vouchers), and the second redirects private funds from taxpayer donations (similar to tax-credit scholarships). The five ESA programs that are currently active serve an estimated 18,706 recipients in the United States. Florida makes up the largest share of that figure, with 11,917 students using an ESA as of fall 2018.[29]

The Promise of ESAs

ESAs have much promise as a policy. If embraced, they have the potential to truly transform our current ossified school system. ESAs give parents the opportunity to personalize learning to the utmost degree, serve students with special needs who require a number of different services, harness the power of technology, bring more school choice to rural areas, make homeschooling more affordable, and enable states to more effectively allocate education dollars.

Interestingly, states have no idea what it actually costs to educate a child. On average, our nation spends $12,201 per student for a year of district public schooling.[30] What this average does not reveal is the enormous variation in state spending. On the lower end, Utah, Arizona, Idaho, and Oklahoma spend under $8,000 per student. On the higher end, New York and the District of Columbia spend over $19,000. New York spent a whopping $22,366 per pupil in 2016.[31] You read that right: $22,366 per kid, per year.

Those who say we are spending too much per pupil become political pariahs; those who say we are spending too little have advocated for the increases that inflated these figures to their current levels. A tangential benefit of ESAs is that they provide transparency to the public about how little of the money spent on *schooling* is actually going toward *educating* their children. The six active ESA laws referenced above grant awards that are less than the state's average per-pupil funding. Thus, when a student uses an ESA rather than the funds traditionally allocated for them at their local public school, the state and taxpayers benefit as a whole. Gaps in funding for ESAs range from a difference per pupil of around $2,200 (Mississippi) to $7,000 (Florida).[32]

Consider this hypothetical based on real figures. If New York spends $22,366 per student, that amounts to $581,516 for a class of twenty-six students. Average teacher salaries in New York public schools range from $56,711 (BA, no teaching experience) to $85,794 (MEd, eight or more years' teaching experience).[33] Taking into account fixed costs such as facilities, utilities, and educational materials, there is still an enormous amount of money left over. Of course, many funds flow to pensions and other long-term benefits that public school teachers accrue. That does not change the fact that much of our per-pupil spending (in the states with very high dollar amounts) is not being efficiently allocated.

In addition to their fiscal benefits, ESAs also enable myriad learning opportunities for students. Importantly, ESAs finance options beyond the classic college preparatory track embraced by most public schools. College education is not the right choice for all students. Careers in skilled trades are more lucrative than ever and often provide the potential to create businesses. Many school districts provide opportunities for training in professions ranging from culinary arts to nursing, cosmetology, and law enforcement. Others lack such resources entirely. ESAs follow the students wherever their skills and desires lead them, including vocational and professional education that is often unavailable in traditional school settings.

One of the most attractive features of an ESA is that it truly enables personalized learning. Personalized learning—a current trend in K–12 education—is the movement to customize learning to enhance a child's learning strengths and combat weaknesses. ESAs accomplish this goal of personalization, because families can choose multiple learning options simultaneously.[34] Consider these three hypotheticals:

1. The Jones family sees that Sally is not being challenged in her local public school due to large class sizes. Moreover, Sally has expressed an interest in learning Arabic and coding due to her future career interests in foreign policy and cybersecurity, though her school does not offer these courses. The Jones family could leverage the power of an ESA to meet all of her learning needs. They could, for example, enroll Sally in a small, technology-focused private school near their home while paying for an Arabic tutor. Alternatively, they could enroll her in a larger, more inexpensive private school that offers Arabic and use any additional funds in the ESA to pay for an online coding class. In other words, parents are empowered to customize their child's education, allocating more efficiently the funds that would be spent on their child in the local public school district.

2. Mr. Reyes is a single parent homeschooling his son Juan in a rural area. He teaches English at a local college and has an advanced degree in English literature. He has been able to homeschool Juan through middle school but fears that the demands of high school chemistry, biology, and environmental science will be outside of his realm of expertise. He has considered enrolling Juan in public school, but it is many miles from their house and doesn't provide the rigor of English instruction that Mr. Reyes could himself provide. There are no private or charter schools in the area. Mr. Reyes could leverage the power of an ESA to pay for online science tutorials, distance-learning classes at a private school in the state capital, many miles away, or once-a-

week science tutoring for Juan, while continuing to provide homeschooling in the humanities.

3. The Roberts family has had four children happily pass through their local public schools and has a currently enrolled fifth child, Darius, with special needs. Mr. and Mrs. Roberts are pleased with the services Darius has received at the local public school, but Darius has expressed a wish to seek employment at a local business after graduation. The nature of Darius's Down syndrome requires that he receive additional coaching in workplace skills so that he is able to seek gainful employment at this local business. The Roberts family may leverage the ESA Darius receives for his special-needs condition to pay for training offered at a local community college in those specific workforce skills. They could combine that with targeted behavioral coaching to ensure that Darius is poised for success in his job.

A child's learning needs, family situation, geographical location, and future aspirations vary widely. Why should they receive a one-size-fits-all education? Whether it is catching up to their peers, advancing in a particular subject, or learning a skill set for emerging careers that is not yet being taught in most schools (such as robotics or coding), ESAs can help. ESAs transfer power to the consumers of education—parents and children—enabling them to choose the combination of schooling opportunities they desire.

ESAs in Action

Individual states, appropriately called "laboratories of democracy" by US Supreme Court justice Louis Brandeis, are beginning to pass ESA policies to serve their citizens. The policies vary in whom they serve, as well as how they are funded, administered, and held accountable. Overall, most states that have successfully passed ESAs have targeted special-needs children first. Raising a differently abled child often can require a battery of services beyond (or in addition to) the traditional public school system. The needs of these children and their families are best served through the variation and specialization an ESA affords. The only commonality among states is that students must have attended a public school for at least one hundred days in the prior school year to receive an ESA. Beyond that, pretty much all of their rules differ.

Eligibility. Florida's education savings account program is open only to children with special needs, and Mississippi's to those with an individualized education plan (IEP).[35] From 2011 to 2017, Arizona's ESA was available to a range of children: those with special needs, adopted children, children of active-duty military, children assigned to failing public schools, Native American children living on tribal lands, siblings of existing account holders, and incoming kindergarteners meeting any of these conditions.[36] In 2017, Governor Doug Ducey signed a bill authorizing its expansion to all Arizona students by 2021, but voters vetoed the bill via ballot measure in 2018.[37] North Carolina's program, similar to Arizona's, is open to special-needs students, those in foster care, and those in active-duty military families. Tennessee's ESA, passed in May 2019, is open to eligible students in the high-need areas of Nashville and Memphis. Nevada's program, though currently inactive due to a funding stalemate in the legislature, is the nation's only *universal* ESA program, open to all students attending public schools in the state.[38]

Funding. In terms of funding, most states with ESAs have chosen to fund them through public coffers, though the private funding method is less open to bureaucratic red tape. As with eligibility, funding levels vary by state. Tennessee's new program will give students the generous sum of $7,300 per year. Mississippi caps student funds at the amount allocated for that special-needs student to attend public school, which amounts to about $6,500 per pupil.[39] For poor children, Arizona's account amount is 100 percent of what would have been spent on that child at their local district or charter school. All other students are funded at 90 percent of the per-student base funding. This amounted to about $5,600 for students without special needs in 2016–17. Students with special needs are eligible for additional funding, depending on what that student's disability requires.[40] Though not currently funded, Nevada's ESA funding mechanism and amount are similar to Arizona's; poor students or those with special needs can receive account payments equal to 100 percent of the statewide funding per pupil (around $6,000), and all other students can receive up to 90 percent of the statewide funding per pupil.[41] Florida's ESA is funded through a General Appropriations Act that specifies a dollar amount for a pot of money annually. The Florida legislature appropriated $128.3 million to this program for 2018–19. Awards to individual students vary by grade, county, and public school spending for students with disabilities.[42] Similar to Florida, North Carolina's legislature appropriated a pot of money—$3.4 million—for the 2018–19 school year, with a maximum value of $9,000 per student per year.[43]

Administration. Interestingly, all states but Florida involve the state Department of Education in administration of ESAs. Experts say that Florida's approach of using a third-party nonprofit is best practice.[44] Such organizations have "greater autonomy and flexibility than state bureaucracies and are primarily dedicated to ensuring that children have access to the educational options they need," according to EdChoice.[45]

ESA Operation and Accountability. As with funding and administration, the operation of each state's ESA is slightly different. Arizona provides funds up front through a prepaid debit card funded quarterly,[46] while Florida, Mississippi, North Carolina, and Tennessee require parents to make purchases out of pocket and seek reimbursement. For low-income families without dependable disposable income, this could make ESAs daunting. To avoid potential problems, Florida's nonprofit developed a payment process for parents who cannot make purchases out of pocket. All states publish a list of lawful learning expenses and require families to send their receipts to the Department of Education quarterly. It is only after these transactions are verified by the auditing agency that the next quarter's deposit is available. In the event of fraud, state officials can close an account immediately. Arizona's auditor reported in 2016 that the state closed 1.2 percent of total account awards due to misuse.[47]

Though inactive, Nevada has the most revolutionary model for processing ESA funds. This system substantially reduces the administrative burden relative to other programs by circumventing the remitting of receipts. Similar to a health savings account, an approved education provider (school or tutor) files a claim with a payment portal called Benefit Wallet. The portal has a master list of approved providers, effectively eliminating the possibility of fraud. The Treasurer's Office gives Benefit Wallet a lump sum quarterly for ESA expenses, and any claim filed by a provider is then paid directly from the parent's Benefit Wallet.[48] It is unclear when, or if, the Nevada program will be funded, but it provides many children with the opportunity to personalize their education in ways unimaginable within the current system.

Ask the Primary Educators

Education savings accounts are so new and so few that it is difficult to find comprehensive empirical studies that do justice to their impact. Yet parents report high levels of satisfaction with the various programs and also reveal their spending preferences when prompted.

Two studies of Arizona parents using an ESA, one conducted in 2013 and another in 2016, found that 71 percent of families are "highly satisfied" with the program. Parents noted that they were able to spend more money on tutoring, and 28 percent said they customized their child's education.[49] Additionally, a 2019 study in Nevada finds that, when provided with a with an explanation of what the ESA is and does, 74 percent of Nevadans favor the state's ESA program.[50]

The setbacks to ESAs in Arizona actually underscore their transformative potential: far more than any other education reform, they transfer power from those who currently possess it (politicians, bureaucracies, and special-interest groups) to those who lack it (parents and service providers). This powerful institutional inertia and resistance underscore the need to couple choice-based reforms with structural reforms within the public schools, to allow principals and teachers to reap the autonomy benefits of family-directed funding.

A Double Standard

A double standard exists over criticism of ESA programs. ESA opponents often argue that that these programs are not held accountable for how money is spent. "Parents spent $700K in school voucher money on beauty supplies, apparel; attempted cash withdrawals" reads a 2018 *Arizona Republic* headline.[51] Although the misspending was alarming, the reporting on Arizona's ESA was incomplete.[52] Matt Beienburg writes for the Goldwater Institute writes that among the culprits was:

> One ESA grandparent . . . buying educational games and supplies for her special-needs grandson that weren't explicitly required by his at-home curriculum and thus not approved under the program . . . and in one case, an ESA parent learned she had earned herself a spot among the highlighted culprits featured in the Auditor General report for having had her card *stolen* and used to purchase cosmetics and clothes. Fraud? Most definitely. A sign of a failed program? Not so much.[53]

The reported misspending totaled about 1 percent of the program's $60 million. When examples like those mentioned above are removed from that figure, the incidence of actual fraud is even smaller. Ironically, the potential for fraud could have been reduced even further, as the program's expansion (subsequently nullified by voters) included a provision to strengthen accountability and transparency.

The media and opponents of choice have an incentive to be critical of ESAs; what they don't acknowledge is that they are not holding the other schools in their states to remotely as high a standard. Indeed, it is arguable that ESA programs are *more* accountable than other forms of schooling. The findings regarding Arizona's ESA program reveal that *more than 99 percent* of ESA funds are used for the education-related expenses for which they are intended. Can school districts, much of whose funding evaporates before it reaches the classroom, say the same about the funding they spend per pupil per year?

ESAs Are the Policy of the Not-So-Distant Future

Education savings accounts are the school choice policy of the future, which no longer seems so distant after the COVID-19 pandemic exposed the inherent inflexibility in many district public school systems. Education savings accounts encourage a prudent distribution of funds on the part of parents, while empowering them to direct the education of their child. This brings society closer to understanding how much it costs to educate a child and how inefficiently their money is currently being spent. And of course, with the structural changes we outlined in prior chapters, schools themselves will be able to determine how these funds are spent, including higher teacher salaries. If embraced, ESAs will enable home and virtual schooling at scale, while allowing children to cultivate and pursue passions. ESAs recognize that no two children are the same; rather, their educational strengths and needs differ.

We conclude this chapter with an important note: none of the proposals we have made anywhere in this book require any students to abandon the schools they love. To the contrary, wherever students go—or remain—the schools will be rewarded with the resources the student commands. Indeed, the sum total of our proposals gives greater power and resources to public schools, while at the same time allowing alternatives. One of the authors is the product of a fantastic suburban traditional public school. Education there was standard but solid, and opportunities for challenge via AP programs and extracurriculars existed. Schools such as these will not, and should not, be discounted or disparaged in discussions about broadening options. Similarly, we recognize that many schools are important mechanisms of food and shelter for low-income students. Those schools should continue to provide those services—and be empowered and funded to provide them even better. But we are not reaping the full return on our educational investment. We should not fear choice and competition in education; indeed, as in nearly every other realm of our lives, we should embrace them. At the same time, the schools in which the vast majority of students are enrolled must be empowered to fulfill their vital educational missions. We should fight for systemic reform in traditional public schools even as we enable options both inside and outside of the public sector. If our goal is providing high-quality educational options to every child, we should never limit the realm of the possible.

CHAPTER 7

The Technology Revolution in Learning

If you've been anywhere near a school in the last few years, you've likely heard the phrases "educational technology," "blended learning," "one-to-one devices," or "personalized learning." It goes without saying that technology and the internet have permanently altered our society; the raging debates surrounding their use have permeated schools as well. Technology is sometimes hailed as a panacea for any number of issues, but it is not. Like all tools, it depends how it is used.

Technology has the power to be a transformative "disruptive innovation," because it brings a good or service (in our case, education) to a population that could not access it, in ways that were previously unimaginable.[1] Before the internet and the proliferation of free learning it makes available, education (especially the free variety) was not available as readily or in such great quantity.

Today, via the internet, the most gifted teachers can provide instruction to far greater numbers of students with minimal cost. A poor student in rural Nebraska with access to the web can learn science from videos made by an Ivy League professor. Through educational technology, student-to-teacher ratios shift from twenty-to-one to ten-million-to-one. Free resources such as Khan Academy illustrate the amazing potential for educational technology, as do language-learning websites such as Duolingo and test preparation modules such as those provided through Modern States. Millions of children (and adults) have learned through these low-cost, clear, and concise modules. In many ways, the internet ensures that we can be lifelong learners of any subject.

Coauthor Bolick did not contribute to this chapter.

Schools should still preserve the interpersonal aspects of students working in groups to solve problems, as this remains much of the human and workplace experience. With the help of technology, these problems can be made appropriately complex or scaled down, based on what each student needs. Real-time assessment, offered by a number of software programs, helps teachers adjust in the moment to ensure that students are mastering the material. Gone are the days of hand-grading for one hundred or more students, a practice that often takes too long to deliver any meaningful formative feedback. Artificial intelligence can be deployed to handle such tasks, as well as to determine a student's level of mastery and tailor learning to individual skills.

Technological innovations such as personalized learning software must be allowed to transform the marketplace of education. In large part, schools have mostly crammed new technologies into their preexisting structure. Technology that assesses each student's learning level and tailors instruction appropriately could mean the difference between catching students up to grade level or leaving them behind. The days of one teacher providing monolithic instruction to the median student should be behind us, thanks to technology.

Educational Technology as a Disruptive Innovation

Education is poised for an enormous disruption, and the COVID-19 pandemic may well have just triggered it. New York governor Andrew Cuomo, in announcing a new partnership with the Gates Foundation to "reimagine" education, emphasized that distance learning may replace the traditional classroom for some students.[2] If that is the case, we had better get serious about harnessing the power of technology for good. The only reason the system has not yet felt the full effects of technology is because of its shackles and disparities in access. The late Harvard business professor Clayton Christensen coined the phrase "disruptive innovation" in the early 1990s, and today it has arrived in education. More than merely a force that makes a good product better, disruptive innovation is the process by which a product or service is made more accessible and affordable to a larger population.[3] That often means substantially changing how services have been provided for a very long time (think the telephone monopoly, airline and banking deregulation, Amazon, and on and on).

As we will discuss, technology makes higher-quality education available to many more people today than ever before. It can also help provide higher-order skills, such as problem solving, creativity, and collaboration, which are increasingly essential in a twenty-first-century economy. Those are the types of skills tested on the international PISA test, on which American students often fall short compared to their peers in other countries.

More Devices, More Change?

This chapter outlines the transformational power of technology as applied to education. It is worth emphasizing, though, that technology is a tool. Like all good tools, it matters how it is used. With the advent of affordable handheld devices, many schools jumped on the tech train and purchased a screen to put in the hands of each student. Yet schools are beginning to wake up to the fact that replacing a book with a laptop does not automatically have the intended effect of improving learning outcomes. Worse, the increasing number of devices in schools has parents up in arms that their children are spending too much time in front of a screen rather than interacting with real people.[4]

The model known as SAMR is helpful in understanding why the addition of more devices has not led to more change. SAMR consists of four steps, beginning with substitution at the lowest level, augmentation at the next level, modification after that, and finally redefinition.

SAMR is a model that schools *should* use to teach teachers about the use of technology in their classrooms. Technology should not be put in student hands without adequate training for teachers. Schools otherwise run the risk that teachers may be manipulated by their more tech-savvy charges.[5]

Unfortunately, most schools are stuck at the lower levels of substitution or augmentation. Think of it like this: if students are given laptops but use them for taking notes, they essentially function as more expensive notebooks (with higher potential for distraction). Laptops in that case act as a direct tool

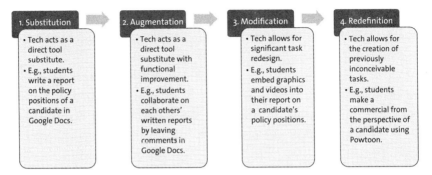

FIGURE 2.   SAMR model. *Source:* Kate J. Hardiman

substitute. By contrast, employing technology as redefinition allows for the creation of new, previously inconceivable, tasks for students. Most important, technology enables previously inconceivable modes and mechanisms of learning.

Technology and the Rise of Personalized Learning in Schools

Technology, as it is currently used in schools, can be loosely grouped into four categories: adaptive, interactive, creative, and simplifying.

"Adaptive software" refers to any technological tool that learns with students—that is, adjusts the questions it provides as they are in the process of answering. Truly reflecting the R (redefinition) level on the SAMR scale, adaptive software has the capability to personalize learning for students in previously unimaginable ways.

Researchers have distilled adaptive software into three categories: adaptive content (which gives students feedback on their specific mistakes when they get something wrong); adaptive assessment (which changes the questions a student sees based on previous responses); and adaptive sequence (which continuously collects and analyzes student data to tailor the skills and content a student encounters next).[6] Essentially, these software programs provide students with individualized support, meet each student at his or her current skill level, and are a step beyond the practice of one teacher teaching the same material to all students at the same time. Teachers can monitor student progress in real time to provide additional feedback to students, and all student data is stored for progress monitoring.

From the teacher perspective, adaptive software gives students nearly constant feedback by leveraging artificial intelligence, something a human teacher is simply unable to do for all students at all times. Above all, adaptive technology shifts the teacher to a role of "guide-on-the-side"—someone who can individually work with students as they struggle to master a concept—rather than the "sage-on-the-stage" who presents the concept to them monolithically.

Interactive Software

Interactive software helps teachers engage students in new ways through technology. Free plug-ins such as Pear Deck give educators and presenters of any kind the power to embed questions into a Google Slides presentation. While the lecture is ongoing, students can respond to questions in real time. From multiple choice to short answer to labeling maps to drawing a concept, Pear Deck revolutionizes classroom lectures in many ways. Rather than waiting for students to raise their hands and calling on the few who always do, teachers can mandate constant participation from all students with Pear Deck. To spark discussion or thoughtful critique of one another's ideas, teachers can even project responses anonymously for all students to view.

Poll Everywhere is a similar tool. This allows presenters to project a question and see audience responses in real time. A great starting point to take the class's pulse on a topic, spark debate, or review, Poll Everywhere has many beneficial uses. Poll questions can take a variety of formats, and all of the data is saved for later review.

Creative Software

Creative software calls on students to expand the way they present their understanding of a concept. Twenty-first-century skills and literacies are often discussed in schools of education for teachers, but what are these really? These skills include (among others) creativity, collaboration, visual presentation, vocal presentation, video creation and editing, and multimedia design.

A number of software programs engage students' creativity while also building complex problem-solving ability and flexibility. Canva, a free website for graphic design, is ideal for a visually stunning presentation of information. Instruction from a teacher, coupled with this software, can help students learn basic principles of marketing and graphic design. Learning Canva's ins and outs empowers students to design professional-looking flyers, posters, and invitations.

Simplifying Software

Simplifying software makes the lives of students, teachers, and parents easier. It improves communication among these three crucial groups, minimizes rote tasks for teachers, and helps teachers monitor their students' progress to ensure that they are on track.

Learning management systems (sometimes abbreviated LMS), such as Schoology, streamline many tasks. Schoology allows teachers to push content to students, message parents of struggling students with ease, and organize course materials in color-coded folders—digitally. Gone are the days of collecting papers from students, losing a few in the process, and forgetting who turned what in when. When students submit an assignment through Schoology, it is time-stamped and collected in one place for easy grading. Teachers can create tests and quizzes right on the platform, saving hundreds of hours of grading. While writing the assessment, teachers select the correct answers for multiple-choice questions, which the software then automatically grades when students submit their work. Open-ended questions can be coded as "subjective," and the teacher can grade all students' responses by question (batch-grade) after all students have submitted. Best of all, the assessment score is then directly imported into the grade book, where all other student grades, attendance, and parent contact information are stored.

After reading about Schoology, you might be wondering how teachers can give tests, quizzes, and other assignments on student devices without worrying that they may look up answers online. Be not afraid: this is where device management software—such as Hapara—enters the picture. Device management software gives teachers unprecedented ability to supervise their students. Teachers can monitor student tabs, documents, and emails, and restrict what websites are accessed. While administering online assessments through Schoology, Google Forms, or another website, teachers can lock their students' devices to the test page until testing ends.

The vast and ever-expanding potential for technology to expand educational opportunities must inform, in a very big way, how teachers are trained. We need not only tech-savvy teachers in all subjects and grades but also (as COVID-19 demonstrated) teachers who are able to quickly adapt and effectively use technological tools such as distance learning. To the extent that we continue to use schools of education to prepare most public school teachers, curricula need to reflect the central and growing importance of technology. We should also overcome our aversion to recruiting teachers from the private sector, which generally has embraced technology far more enthusiastically than school bureaucracies have. Teachers should be offered incentives and training to use new technological tools. And parents should be offered training as well. One benefit of funding education through ESAs is expanding the universe of families who can afford to access technological tools and the hardware necessary to access them. And by decentralizing decision making in public schools, principals and teachers can choose to devote more resources to technology.

Understanding all the ways technology can personalize learning in schools is no small feat. Yet much unexplored and untapped potential exists for these devices to truly improve learning. With the right understanding, teachers can help students become responsible and savvy digital users.

Technology and the Rise of Homeschooling

Educational technology also enables homeschooling, which ironically was the fastest-growing form of education in the United States even before the COVID-19 pandemic. But with the mandatory closure of nearly every school in the nation, most families had only two options: homeschooling or no schooling at all. Corey DeAngelis, who directs school choice policy at the Reason Foundation, points out that during the pandemic, "millions of families that previously sent their children to government schools are now getting to test-drive some form of home education."[7]

Many will never want to do full-time home education again. Others may have discovered useful ways to supplement their children's in-school education. Still others may find homeschooling to be preferable to their previous school environment. Interestingly, a RealClear Opinion Research poll of 2,122 registered voters found that 40 percent of families are more likely to choose homeschooling or virtual school enrollment after the lockdowns end. Additionally, 64 percent of the same group said they support school choice in some form.[8]

Favorable anecdotal reports abound as well. Veronique Mintz, a thirteen-year-old from New York City, took to the pages of the *New York Times* to extol the advantages of distance learning over her previous middle school experience. After roughly a month of distance learning, she wrote, "I find that I am learning more, and with greater ease, than when I attended regular classes. I can work at my own pace without being interrupted by disruptive students and teachers who seem unable to manage them."[9] Even if only 2 percent of public school families continue to teach their children at home, whether for fear of the virus or as a matter of educational preference, it would add one million children to homeschooling ranks.[10]

Yet we emphatically emphasize that the forced, emergency home-based education during the pandemic *is not representative of true homeschooling*. First, the mandatory diversion to distance learning violates our maxim that if you like your school, you can keep it. Second, it was forced on families for whom it was totally impracticable—those with two working parents, those who do not speak English as their first language, and those whose school districts do not have the technology to provide children with devices to connect with teachers on a regular basis. Yet, as this section demonstrates, there is great promise for the future of *true* homeschooling. It may even find new adherents in those who had positive experiences during the pandemic's crash course.

The replacement of traditional schooling with homeschooling during the pandemic did not provide much of a glimpse into the variations available. Typically, school districts provided lessons or materials online, and it was up to parents and students to keep pace. Many parents, owing to work or other responsibilities, do not have the time to help organize, monitor, and support their children's lessons. But of the available distance-learning options—many of them provided by charter operators like K12 and Primavera, and even some offered by school districts—many provide comprehensive learning experiences that do not require extensive parental involvement.[11] Schools like K12 offer online learning services to traditional public schools. In some school districts, homeschoolers are allowed to purchase discrete services, such as chemistry labs and extracurricular activities, thus creating a hybrid education and providing extra resources for public schools.

One online school, Florida Virtual School, has provided learning opportunities in all fifty states. It offers more than 190 courses, with progress measured not in fixed academic years but by course completion, which allows the school to customize education for each student. The school offers more than fifty clubs and numerous virtual events and arranges trips domestically and abroad for students to interact in person and explore new experiences. As many school districts struggled to meet the challenges of online learning forced upon them by the pandemic, many enlisted Florida Virtual Schools, which grew from 215,000 students in 2019 to 2.7 million by spring 2020.[12] In this way, a very old idea—homeschooling—was able to harness technology to help meet an unprecedented educational crisis.

Homeschooling Origins

The concept of homeschooling has been around since the advent of education, though it was mainly a privilege of the elite who could afford private tutors. American education theorists John Holt and Raymond Moore extolled the value of homeschooling and sought to normalize the practice in the 1970s. Holt pushed back against the industrial one-size-fits-all model of schooling for children, advocating for "unschooling," while Moore was concerned about psychological and moral formation. In the 1980s, evangelical and fundamentalist Christian parents entered the movement, pushing back against the increasing secularization of public schools.[13]

As a young attorney in Colorado in the 1980s, I provided pro bono legal services to homeschoolers, many of whom were still being criminally prosecuted around the country. I find it a remarkable sign of progress that homeschooling today is widely accepted, even among Ivy League universities, which welcome homeschooled students.

It is difficult to know precisely how many children are homeschooled in the United States in a given year. Data from the National Center for Education Statistics[14] and analyses by researcher Brian Ray suggest that the number of homeschooled children is growing by 2 to 8 percent each year. Between 1999 to 2012, the percentage of homeschooled students doubled from 1.7 to 3.4 percent of the school-age population. The most recent nationwide data estimated that 2.5 million students (ages 5–17) are homeschooled.[15] Astonishingly, this means that the number of homeschooled students will soon surpass the 2.5 million students enrolled in charter schools.

Yet homeschooling does not receive nearly the attention it deserves from those seeking to reform the American education system. Homeschooling has a distinct advantage over other reforms: it is the only movement within education that unites those on all sides of the political, pedagogical, and religious spectrums. We seek to explain who is homeschooling (past and present), why they are choosing to do so, the potential value of a home-based education, and the policy levers able to make this a reality for more families.

Who Homeschools?

Here's a great trivia question: What do inner-city Black cultural enthusiasts, suburban middle-class Catholics, and Silicon Valley techies have in common? The answer: almost nothing, except that members of these groups are homeschooling their children. Though traditionally labeled as the choice of conservative religious parents with antisocial children, homeschooling defies that stereotype today.

In 2016, researchers from the National Center for Education Statistics (NCES) calculated that homeschoolers fell into the following demographic categories: 59 percent were white, 26 percent Hispanic, 8 percent Black, and 7 percent Asian or Pacific Islander. Though the percentage of homeschooled students who are white decreased from 68 percent in 2012 to 59 percent in 2016, the percentage of homeschooled students who are Hispanic increased by 11 percent over the same time frame. This percentage increase amounts to the difference between 250,000 Hispanic students in 2012 to just under 450,000 in 2016.[16] Though it is unclear what is driving the increase in Hispanic home-schooling, the NCES survey found that 11 percent of families homeschooling do not have a parent who speaks English. Interestingly, the highest rate of homeschooling in 2016 happened in households in which parents had not completed high school, followed by parents who had completed bachelor's degrees. A comparatively smaller number of parents with graduate and professional degrees are choosing to homeschool their children.[17]

Interestingly, the NCES also found in 2016 that homeschooled students were more likely than other students to live below the poverty line—disproving the stereotype that homeschooling is a privilege of the affluent. Indeed, it may well be that it is a recourse for the poor trapped in failing school districts. Finally, homeschoolers are located in rural, urban, and suburban areas at rates similar to other students. Their geographic distribution suggests that home-schooling is not primarily motivated by distance to school or lack of educational options, as these abound in cities.

Even more telling than statistics about homeschoolers are their stories; we turn to these next.

Education as Liberation

Though the percentage of homeschooled students who are Black appears relatively low, this demographic group has compelling reasons for home-based education. Baltimore mother April VaiVai views homeschooling as a way to protect her daughter from racial inequality in the inner-city schools.[18] Federal data show that Black students are nearly four times as likely as their white classmates to be suspended from school.[19] Moreover, Black students (due to residential segregation) tend to attend schools that receive less funding from local property taxes, have less access to high-rigor courses such as AP or STEM (science, technology, engineering, and math), and have twice as many teachers lacking subject-matter expertise and teaching experience.[20]

VaiVai views homeschooling as an effective counter to all of these disparities, as well as a way to hold her daughter to high expectations. For VaiVai, culture is also key. At home, she is able to emphasize the tradition of Black excellence in America and the cultural traditions of the African diaspora, teachings often not included in traditional schools' curriculum.[21] In a poignant sense, the "radical self-reliance" of Black homeschooling echoes the history of freed slaves in America, who viewed education as a means of liberation for their children. It is crushing, however, that our public education system has failed them so dramatically that they are driven to take matters into their own hands.

Support groups such as National Black Home Educators seek to encourage and mentor Black families choosing to homeschool. Their website provides curriculum resources, explains the various webs of local and state support groups, offers classes in life skills, and advertises regular homeschooler field trip events to forge family-to-family connection. The stated purpose of their organization even extends beyond education: it is "ultimately to see strong families with healthy parent child relationships."[22]

A Bilingual Approach

Homeschooling among Hispanic families is growing at a rapid rate. Like all other parents, Hispanics have varied reasons for homeschooling; a main one is the desire to provide a bilingual education. Homeschooling mom Monica Olivera runs the blog *Mommy Maestra*, through which she shares experiences, reading materials, and curriculum for Latino homeschoolers. Olivera poignantly writes, "As a Latina, I also feel the overwhelming desire to raise my children to be bilingual and bicultural. . . . In addition to learning the language, I also strive to find ways to supplement our curriculum with cultural books, activities and themes that reflect the richness of our heritage. . . . We live in a small farming community, with no immersion schools or Spanish programs for small children available. So their bilingualism and biculturalism rests on my shoulders."[23] Olivera also notes that her decision to homeschool was initially driven by the fact that her children were zoned to a "failed school district," where the state took over and closed two schools.

Other than anecdotal evidence, the research is almost nil on Latino homeschooling families.[24] Most studies lump in this demographic group with African American and other nonwhite groups when studying reasons for homeschooling and their outcomes. However, much like Black students, Latino students face marginalization in inner-city public schools and access to fewer resources than their white peers. The education they receive in school may simply not be enough for students who are English language learners. Younger bilingual students benefit across subjects from learning in both their native language and English until they reach proficiency in both. Yet often they are taught only how to advance their English language skills rather than learning other important content.[25]

Start-Up Education

Successful tech start-ups have always resisted the traditional way of doing things, launching projects in a garage (Apple) or a college dorm room (Facebook), for example. Tech-sector families are similarly bucking the traditional education system by homeschooling their children. Known for their entrepreneurial spirit, preference for remote work, and creativity, parents working in the technology sector are natural homeschoolers. "The world is changing. It's looking for people who are creative and entrepreneurial, and that's not going to happen in a system that tells kids what to do all day," California homeschooling parent Samantha Matalone Cook stated. She and her husband, Chris, a lead systems administrator at Pandora, are vocal supporters of homeschooling.[26] Matalone Cook also writes a blog about homeschooling her two boys with a focus on technology and creativity. Additionally, she mentors a group of four- to seven-year-old hackers who are "working on a robotics project, using the technology we learned from completing brush bots and art bots to create robots that will go over a variety of surfaces."[27] Not exactly your average kindergarten classroom.

Lisa Betts-LaCroix, another California mother, started a homeschooling group called Bay Area Gifted Home Educators, which now includes more than four hundred families. Betts-LaCroix said a growing number are tech entrepreneurs.[28] She resists the term *homeschooling*, preferring instead to call this new form of education "a revolution." Betts-LaCroix emphasizes that the students in her group do anything *but* stay at home: the group partners with a number of local organizations, including museums, San Francisco Shakespeare, and environmental groups to provide community-based learning experiences. "I do believe that we are going to be lifelong learners in the future," Betts-LaCroix stated. "I believe we're going to be needing to re-create ourselves all the time. When the world is moving as quickly as it is and changing as quickly as it is, we're all going to need to learn new skill sets."[29] According to Betts-LaCroix and other parents in the group, homeschooling revamped best inspires these qualities of lifelong learning and adaptability.

Interestingly, these families are leveraging public charter schools in their area that offer independent study for children. This allows them to access the state funds that would typically flow to those schools if their children were to enroll as traditional classroom students. Eight such schools currently exist in the San Francisco Bay Area, and more are sure to spring up if this movement continues to grow. We discuss this fruitful ground for incentivizing homeschooling at the conclusion of this chapter.

Back to Basics, Hybrid Style

The final model we have chosen to profile most closely resembles the stereotypical version of homeschooling to pass along religious beliefs—with a twist. Regina Caeli, Latin for Queen of Heaven, is an inventive model that blends three days of classic Catholic homeschooling curriculum with two days of teacher-led classroom Socratic seminar. It satisfies Catholic families' desire to inculcate the faith for a fraction of the cost of private school. Regina Caeli has expanded rapidly since its advent in 2014, to serve pre-K through twelfth-grade students in twelve locations for less than $4,000 per student per year (about one-fourth of the national average per-pupil public school expenditure). This educational model prioritizes teaching values and virtues as well as content, including joy, peace, courage, kindness, wisdom, fidelity, prudence, and self-control. Its founders believe that its model "fosters the joy all children can experience in learning," "promotes peace in the home by supporting homeschool families," and helps "families find the moral courage to be 'in the world, but not of the world.'"

Regina Caeli's students study the intellectual tradition of the classical liberal arts, "so that the great thinkers and authors of the last 2,500 years become their teachers." Students begin to study Latin in fourth grade and participate in faith formation within the Catholic tradition. Students also have the opportunity to study abroad, learning about the richness of the Catholic faith through an "educationally and spiritually enriching pilgrimage" to Italy. Finally, students in tenth grade or above may earn dual credit at Holy Apostles Catholic College—for one-third the normal college tuition.[30]

Why Homeschool?

The reasons are as varied as the stories we just described. The best thing about homeschooling—and what makes it distinct as a form of education—is that it looks different for every family, child, and context. We have mentioned a limited sample of countless unique homeschooling narratives. Homeschooling theorist John Holt understood as early as the 1970s that varied reasons for this type of education exist. He wrote in the periodical *Growing without Schooling*,

> Those who . . . want to take or keep their children out of schools, may have very different, in some cases opposed reasons for doing this. Some may feel that the schools spend too much time on what they call the Basics; others that they don't spend enough. Some may feel that the schools teach a dog-eat-dog competitiveness; others that they teach a mealy-mouth Socialism. Some may feel that the schools teach too much religion; other that they don't teach enough but teach instead a shallow atheistic humanism. I think the schools degrade both science and religion, and do not encourage either strong faith or strong critical thought.[31]

Data found through National Household Education Surveys (NHES), though not as moving as the individual stories, reveal additional information about the preferences of homeschooling parents. When asked about the most important factor in their decision to homeschool, 25 percent said the environment of other schools, 19 percent said the academic instruction at other schools,

16 percent referenced a desire to provide religious instruction, and 21 percent checked "other." When parents could check numerous options beyond their "most important" reason, nine in ten reported that concern about school environments was an important motivator (a category that includes "safety, drugs, negative peer pressure" and the like), 77 percent selected the option about moral instruction, 64 percent chose the option about religious instruction, and 74 percent selected a dissatisfaction with the academic instruction at other schools.[32] This nationally representative survey suggests that families have multiple reasons to homeschool. As the stories illustrate, some families' main reasons slip through the data's cracks.

Cracks in the Data

Some "use statistics as a drunk man uses lamp-posts—for support rather than for illumination," Scottish poet Andrew Lang quipped. Statistics about homeschooling are valuable to *support* an understanding of which families choose this option and why, but they do not fully *illuminate* this interesting trend. The data may miss other notable issues in education that parents wish to escape.

The first is, quite simply, that we are crushing young minds with standardized test preparation. In the past, students had the opportunity to engage with rigorous academics, the arts, music, free play, and physical activity at school. Today, we train them to take tests so that we can sort them into proficiency categories—a practice that serves only to continually tell us with hard data that our education system is failing. Though testing is important for accountability purposes and to measure student growth, it is not the end of education in itself.

A second, related point is that we are boring our children. Education advocate Ken Robinson discusses this at length in his often-cited Ted Talk "Do Schools Kill Creativity?"[33]

A third factor is the belief that public schools inculcate values that are fundamentally different from those of many parents. In our constitutional republic, parents retain the fundamental right and obligation to provide for the education, values, and character of their children.[34]

We now consider each factor as a potential motivator for homeschooling.

Though standardized tests seem like a fixture in American education, testing did not truly become a focus in schools until the federal government's 2001 No Child Left Behind initiative. Harvard professor Daniel Koretz writes in his new book, *The Testing Charade*, that our system's focus on testing is only "pretending to make schools better."[35] Schools are spending immense amounts of time and money prepping kids for tests. A comprehensive study of sixty-six big-city school districts found that students spend between twenty and twenty-five hours taking tests each year and countless more preparing. Between pre-K and twelfth grade, students in traditional public schools take about 112 mandatory standardized exams, to the tune of about $1.7 billion per year.[36] Arguing that test prep in schools actually inflates test scores and incentivizes cheating (primarily on behalf of the adults in the system), Koretz believes it has hurt more than it has helped. It is widely documented that parents—and students—are revolting against standardized testing.[37] More parents, and their children, may begin to view homeschooling as a viable way to avoid the testing focus in schools.

The rise of testing has concurrently quashed creativity, according to education advocates and numerous teachers who have written on this issue. Robinson emphasized in "Do Schools Kill Creativity?" that education is meant to take us into an unknown future of life and work.[38] He posits that "creativity is as important as literacy" but that our ingrained conception of education (and the standardized tests it foists upon children) only value reading and math. Similarly, Denver English teacher Don Batt writes that on standardized tests "the children are asked which answer is right, although the smarter children realize that sometimes there are parts of several answers that could be right. And they sit. And they write. Not to express their understanding of the world. Or even to form their own opinions. . . . Instead they must dance the steps that they have been told are important. . . . What do they learn? That school is torture. That learning is drudgery."[39]

Good teachers who adopt a personalized approach to learning, including homeschooling parents, may assess students' abilities in myriad creative ways. Though homeschooling students should be held accountable, as all other students are, through a norm-referenced test, parents who do not want testing to be the focus of their child's education should have the flexibility to pursue alternative models.

Though a dogged focus on testing (and the boredom that results) is a significant issue and a potential driver behind homeschooling, a less-discussed force sweeping public schools is perceived ideological and political indoctrination. Whether the issue is sex education, climate change, or the absence of religion in the schools, many parents object to the values and politics embraced by many public schools. As political institutions, public schools are susceptible to influence from both right and left. Huge battles have taken place over subjects ranging from evolution to gender dysphoria. Textbooks and curricula are usually at the center of such values. Recently, a suburban Alaska school district joined the culture wars by removing six classic books, including *Catch-22*, *I Know Why the Caged Bird Sings*, and *The Great Gatsby*, from its curriculum due to sexual content that was deemed inappropriate.[40] Other districts have implemented sex education programs and teach about sexual orientation in ways that are deeply offensive to many parents.[41] Homeschooling allows families to opt out and direct the values that will guide their children's education and upbringing.

Even teacher certification can be subject to ideological influence. Some programs require a "dispositional analysis" of teaching candidates, a vague criterion that sometimes embraces things such as commitments to "social justice," "diversity," or even a downplaying of American exceptionalism.[42] Graduate student and teaching candidate Ed Swan was assigned to diversity training at Washington State University for expressing his belief that "white privilege and male privilege do not exist." He received negative evaluations as to his "disposition" and was instructed to be "sensitive to community and cultural norms."[43] A similarly controversial University of Minnesota ideological litmus test for future teachers based on "a highly politicized notion of 'cultural competence'" was revised only after a lawsuit.[44]

I was disappointed after reading the magazine of the National Council of Teachers of English in 2019, which reported on the organization's resolutions on such issues as gun control and climate change. Teachers should not be encouraged to politically indoctrinate their students, and it is clear that the magazine assumed a teacher consensus around those issues. The goal of education is to lead students to understand both sides of an issue, without bias, so that they can formulate their own opinions.

KJH

Many parents, whatever their political persuasion, care deeply about the values and political orientation to which their children are exposed. But they are usually ill equipped to fight political battles over curriculum, textbooks, and teacher certification, especially when powerful interest groups on either side of the ideological divide are pursuing their agendas. When parents believe their children are potentially being indoctrinated to toss aside the values that they struggle to impart, they may be motivated to direct their education differently.

Closing Achievement Gaps, Creating Lifelong Learners

For parents choosing to homeschool, their efforts are paying off. While data reveals faltering educational progress for students in traditional public schools, it is thrilling to see the successes of home-based students. According to homeschool researcher Dr. Brian Ray, Black home-educated students scored at or above the national average in all core subjects. In comparison, Black public school students on average scored at or below the thirtieth percentile in the same subjects on the same test. Thus, homeschooling could have implications for narrowing achievement gaps. Gender and socioeconomic status were not significant predictors of this outcome, suggesting that the positive effect is due to the variable of homeschooling itself.[45] More research from Ray and the National Home Education Research Institute reveals that the 2014 SAT scores of college-bound homeschool students were much higher than the national average, including "notably large differences" of 0.61 standard deviations in reading, 0.26 in math, and 0.42 in writing.

Colleges and universities are actively recruiting homeschooled students, including Harvard, Yale, MIT, Stanford, and Duke.[46] Homeschooled students are especially attractive because the model leads them to pursue learning passions, develop motivation, build strong time management skills, and work without distractions. Freedom from the shackles of the structured school day enables all of this and more. Finally, personalized learning—the idea that instruction should be tailored to students' learning preferences, interests, and skill level—is truly possible in homeschooling. In the typical classroom, it is simply a buzzword—the next innovation in education that is challenging for teachers to implement in practice.

Support for homeschooling is increasing as educational paradigms them-selves are changing. We have largely begun the important disassociation between schools and schooling, aided by the readily accessible amount of information on the internet. We are witnessing a revolution; practices and ideas once accepted as givens are now dubious. They include the conventional wisdom that a degree is a guarantee of a better life, that large amounts of stan-dardized test preparation are necessary to achieve such a degree, that school must take place from September to June between the hours of 8 a.m. and 3 p.m., that all students should study the same subjects, and that the one-teacher-one-classroom model is adequate to teach all students. The idea that a parent (or group of parents) could provide a personalized, rigorous, and thoughtfully compiled education from the comfort of home should not shock us in the slightest.

Technology has made high-quality educational opportunities easily acces-sible to families who choose to educate their children, in whole or part, at home. Likewise, funding through ESAs would enable those who lack the financial means to make the same choices. Learning, wherever it takes place, fulfills the goals of public education. Homeschooling is proving its worth as a vital part of our K–12 educational system.

Redefining the Roles of Teacher and Student

Technology applied to education, as we hope to have made clear, has incred-ible potential. Yet technology does not (and will never) have a soul that can care for a child. The teacher as an empathetic, relational being cannot begin to be replaced by technology. However, tactful deployment of technology funda-mentally redefines the roles of teacher and student.

For teachers, it has the potential to minimize rote tasks (namely grading) so that they can put more time into planning and instruction. It has the potential to allow master teachers to reach more students, especially those beyond their classroom. It has the potential to create educational experiences for students that would not have been possible twenty years prior.

For students, learning how to use technology well and responsibly is of the utmost importance. Consider this fascinating description of difference in information transmission today. Before 2000, to learn about any number of things, children were beholden to teachers, parents, access to a local library, community organizations, churches, neighbors, or friends. They had to attend, ask, receive, and store the information given to them by others. Before our modern era of instant information, children received information from key gatekeepers.

Today, children can find everything online. Rather than needing to be in school, in their science classroom, with their credentialed science teacher, at precisely 10:34 on a Tuesday morning, learners can access information whenever, wherever, and for whatever reason they wish to do so. A few simple keystrokes return one thousand potential answers to their question within nanoseconds. Processing the deluge of information available to them, separating what is true from what is biased, exaggerated, or downright false, is the modern student's challenge.

It is here that the new roles of teacher and student converge. Teachers and students must begin to view themselves as allies in a learning process aided by technology. Arguably, we have reached a point at which teens know more about the devices they are given in school than do adults. Technology is a powerful force—if we master it. Teachers need to effectively guide technology use and integrate it into the broader learning experience; if we don't master it, it will master us. A traditional school or homeschool's deployment of technology must be much more sophisticated than placing devices into the hands of every student. What use is technology if students can find information on the internet but have no idea if they have landed upon factual content or an advertisement (and a landmark study shows they cannot)?[47] What use is technology if it serves to distract malleable young brains rather than engage? What use is technology if students lose the ability to talk to one another and cannot build interpersonal and emotional intelligence skills? What use is technology if it only makes the learning process more boring?

Despite its perils, the promise of technology abounds. Many of the technologies described here will be surpassed by new and better ones. The key point is that education today must be technology savvy. Teachers must be trained to use technology in sophisticated ways. Even more, our education policies must promote learning, both in and out of school, that both leverages and mitigates the power of technology.

CHAPTER 8

Allocating Resources Effectively, Enabling Innovative Models

School: desks in rows, one teacher per room, books, single-content-area classes, tests, more tests, the same subjects (with infrequent connections to the real world), the same length school day, the same length school year. The same story from 1919 to 2019. Schools have ossified into this model and are shackled by many of the forces noted in the beginning of this book to remain exactly as they are. It's crucial to keep in mind that when we allow our schools to be shackled, the true recipients of a bad structure are children. Indeed, in many ways our schools are holding our children back from reaching their true potential.

Fortunately, in addition to the substantial public resources invested in public schools, we also have enormous philanthropic resources directed toward education. Much of that investment is made by individuals who have become billionaires in the technology industry. No sector of our economy has a larger stake in American education, for educated young people are essential to filling STEM jobs today and producing new technological discoveries tomorrow. And no sector of our economy is better positioned to bring the lessons of disruptive innovation our education system so desperately needs.

But unfortunately, much of the philanthropic investment is poorly allocated, and few lessons of disruptive innovation are brought to bear. We need the leaders of our technological revolution to lead the education revolution.

In this chapter, we shine a spotlight on several innovative school models. All are breaking the mold of traditional schooling in some way. Some have altered staffing arrangements, others the physical structures of schools. Some have chosen to change what students are learning and how they demonstrate their knowledge. All are exemplary in their own way; all represent twenty-first-century learning and the promise of an unshackled future system. It is these schools that philanthropies should target and help grow. Though there are indications that the winds of philanthropy are shifting this way, the most generous donors continue to throw money at a failed system.

Philanthropic Funding over Time

Philanthropists have given massive amounts of money in an effort to improve K–12 education. Recognizing the need to improve the system and develop skilled high school graduates, technology entrepreneurs like Bill Gates and Mark Zuckerberg have put their money where their mouths are. Yet, despite spending billions of dollars, there is little to show for their efforts. Until recently, their investments have been the antithesis of the innovation and disruptive innovation that made them billionaires. Instead, for the majority of their years of giving, they tinkered around the edges, pouring money into a broken public education system.

Philanthropies have been active in education since the early 1900s. Steel tycoon and philanthropist Andrew Carnegie made the first substantial donation—$2 million—to create a technical school in Pittsburgh. Initially secondary schools created to further "the development of skills and innovations purposely applied to meet real-world needs," the schools eventually merged to form Carnegie Mellon University.[1] Since then, influence over education has slowly shifted from those tied most closely to the project of educating—administrators and teachers—to those with the largest pocketbooks: philanthropists.

The publication of the *Nation at Risk* report in 1983 was an inflection point for the involvement of outside groups in education.[2] The historical moment of the late Cold War era heightened fears raised in this report about the global competitiveness of our next generation. Big money rushed onto the scene shortly thereafter to save the day, with the Annenberg Foundation giving a $500 million donation in 1993. Interestingly, this original donation was for the express purpose of "restructuring public schools," with $400 million pledged "to education organizations and associations engaged in campaigns to overhaul school system bureaucracies and to improve curriculums, teaching and student achievement."[3] In identifying bureaucracy as an impediment to school reform and trusting local groups to lead the change, Walter H. Annenberg was far ahead of his time. Yet, since his generous gift, the bureaucratic machine has only become more entrenched in public education. Annenberg is surely rolling over in his grave.

Observers of the initial gift, and the $1.1 billion that resulted from matching grants, have overwhelmingly expressed disappointment with its results.[4] As Duke law professor and scholar of philanthropies Joel Fleishman writes, "The national challenge was essentially a set of disjointed and inconsistent programs, guided by no overarching strategy, that produced outcomes that were mixed at best."[5] Former US assistant secretary of education Chester Finn's study of the Annenberg donation's impact seven years later tellingly concludes, "Good intentions and a generous checkbook are clearly not enough to transform American education. Short-run innovation can be bought with money, but durable reform takes something more powerful." The Annenberg effort to reform school district bureaucracy, though noble, misunderstood how the major players—teachers' unions, districts, and teacher education programs—work. An Annenberg partner was expected to build relationships with the same bureaucracies it ultimately was there to reform, a self-defeating venture for an outsider, even one with deep pockets.[6] Past giving from Annenberg and modern giving from Zuckerberg demonstrate that working within the system to change the system falls short every time.

The Explosion of Funding at the Turn of the Century

The role of private philanthropies truly exploded in the early 2000s with the entrance of the big three education funders: the Bill and Melinda Gates Foundation, the Walton Family Foundation, and the Eli and Edythe Broad Foundation. They attempted to learn from the Annenberg venture by proactively defining their priorities and setting the agenda for reform. They also realized that pure dollars would not inspire the change that they sought.[7] Analysis of foundation giving over time indicates that these organizations are wielding their checkbooks in different but influential ways.

The increasing federal role in education after the Bush era's No Child Left Behind initiative opened up new avenues for philanthropies to shape policy priorities. Though foundations are precluded by law from engaging in politics, large foundations have shifted their giving toward national research and advocacy over time.[8] In addition to donating directly to specific school districts and states, these philanthropies incentivize policy makers in federal and state governments to adopt their favored strategies. Over time, the foundations have aligned their giving portfolios, allowing them to exert even greater influence.[9] Researcher Sarah Reckhow writes, "Foundations have amplified a new set of voices in national policymaking around this more focused group of issues. This type of coordinated grant-making could accelerate changes to the educational interest group sector at the national level."[10]

But their approaches vary. In addition to supporting innovative public school approaches, the Walton Foundation has invested heavily in charter schools and private school choice, and the Broad Foundation has generously supported charter schools as well. By contrast, the Bill and Melinda Gates Foundation, the biggest of the three, has focused almost exclusively on public schools and national, top-down public policy.

The Gates Foundation's investments in education since 2001 top $6 billion. Over time, the foundation's spending has been directed toward a number of initiatives, the vast majority within district public education. Inspired by the high school graduation and college-readiness rates of smaller schools, the Gates Foundation initially worked to break up large high schools into smaller units.[11] Yet, according to Wharton School statistician Howard Wainer, the foundation may have misunderstood the numbers when making this first donation; small schools are overrepresented at both the low and high ends of the spectrum.[12] Indeed, the smaller the student body, the more likely its metrics are to be skewed by a few strong or a few weak students. In a recent speech, Gates himself admitted that this strategy failed, stating that "the financial costs of closing existing schools and replacing them with new schools was too high."[13] Implied: breaking up unsuccessful large schools into smaller schools did not make them successful.

In one dramatic case, Gates's focus on creating smaller schools actually ended up shutting down a Denver high school.[14] Though Manual High had numerous prior struggles, the Gates grant was seemingly the last straw. The school board gave the breakup the green light in the spring of 2001, effectively separating the school into three separate "learning communities" in the same building. After this, over $1.2 million flowed to the school. Yet by 2006 the school had lost 354 students, and the *Denver Post* wrote that "three feuding principals hoarded textbooks and called police on each other's students."[15] The principals reportedly battled over shared spaces in the building such as the cafeteria, library, and gym. The *Post* cites Children's Campaign estimates that the 2005 dropout rate at Manual was more than 75 percent. Tom Vander Ark, then executive director for education initiatives at the Gates Foundation, ironically commented that, in hindsight, "we would only work with a district that has a strong commitment to get all kids graduating."[16] The Manual example is a sad, shocking testimony to just how wrong some philanthropic ventures, though well intended, may go. This story also underscores how easy it is for foundations to step back from the mess they have created, leaving those in charge to shoulder the blame and pick up the pieces.

After its first set of ventures, the Gates Foundation reoriented its priorities toward standards-based reform in 2009. Giving more than $400 million for the Common Core Standards Initiative and related advocacy, Gates truly went all in with this reform.[17] This particular investment helped bring about one of the most wide-reaching, yet hotly contested, changes in US education to date.[18] The foundation went far beyond bankrolling the initiative. Gates built coalitions of support across the country, persuaded state and local leaders to make sweeping curricular changes, and funded media coverage of the issue. Gates gave money to all sides of the political spectrum—from teachers' unions to the US Chamber of Commerce—impelling the fastest nationwide reform in history.[19] All whom this money reached championed Common Core unreservedly. Progressives and conservatives who had historically disagreed on nearly every issue in education reform suddenly joined the same pro–Common Core team when Gates money was on the table.[20] Indeed, this was the *only* national education reform in history that over forty states and the District of Columbia adopted without awaiting results of field tests or pilot projects.[21]

By 2014, however, states began dropping the national standards as quickly as possible. Test scores displayed little to no improvement, parents and pundits decried "federal meddling" in education, and schools did not understand how to implement the standards.[22] Another external reform foisted on a failing system bites the dust. Gates himself tacitly admitted failure, noting in a speech that "if there is one thing I have learned, it is that no matter how enthusiastic we might be about one approach or another, the decision to go from pilot to wide-scale usage is ultimately and always something that has to be decided by you and others in the field."[23] Hardly a mea culpa, this statement does not mention, as was the case, that Common Core never even had a pilot phase. Gates Foundation CEO Sue Desmond-Hellmann similarly admitted defeat in a letter, writing that "unfortunately our foundation underestimated the level of resources and support required for our public education systems to be well-equipped to implement the standards."[24] Here, Desmond-Hellmann reveals the true misconception philanthropies have of the US public education system: they believe that more resources can always fix the problem. More than twenty-five years of this approach provide a historic lesson: throwing more money at the stultified bureaucracy of a failing system, even under the auspices of different types of reform, will always disappoint.

In 2017, Bill Gates proclaimed that the foundation was back for more. In a speech pledging $1.7 billion over the next five years to aid public education in the United States, he said that the foundation wanted to "move our work closer to the classroom."[25] This likely means more tinkering with Common Core, just at the classroom level rather than on the state or national plane. Disturbingly, in the same speech, Gates stated that "teachers need better curricula and professional development aligned with the Common Core. . . . We are increasing our commitment to develop curricula and professional development aligned to state standards." This implies that the foundation itself, despite lacking knowledge of how to educate, will drive curriculum creation, which then may be indirectly imposed on teachers by Gates pulling on the purse strings. Moreover, only 15 percent of the aforementioned $1.7 billion will flow to charter schools, despite the strong results of many of these schools.[26]

Following Gates's lead, Facebook's Mark Zuckerberg has also given large checks to the US public education system. Zuckerberg's giving, though more concentrated, has also failed to make any noticeable impact. In 2010, he pumped $100 million, with the promise of a $100 million matching grant, into Newark Public Schools in New Jersey. At the time of the investment, Newark's high school graduation rate was 60 percent, 19 points below the national average, and 90 percent of those who did graduate had to take remedial classes before going to the local community college.[27] Mayor Ras Baraka said Zuckerberg's foundation "parachuted in" and didn't engage local groups who had been trying to improve the schools for many years. It is also interesting how Zuckerberg's foundation spent the money. Of the investment, $89.2 million went to labor and contract costs, fueling the teachers' union. Comparatively, $57.6 million went to Newark charter schools, $21 million went to consultants, and $24.6 million went to local initiatives, such as literacy programs.[28] When Zuckerberg's initiative ended after its five promised years, it was largely considered a failure.

A Drop in the Bucket

All told, the United States spends more than $600 billion a year on its traditional public school systems.[29] The massive giving by private individuals only underscores that the system needs greater help than it is already receiving. Yet philanthropic giving, though generous, is merely a drop in the bucket compared to already expended resources. In most cases, private funding amounts to less than half a percent of spending by local, state, and federal governments on education. Though seemingly large on paper, these donations have had dubious results due to the way they are targeted and implemented.

Michael Bailin, then president of the Edna McConnell Clark Foundation, summed up the problem with philanthropic giving to education in a 2003 lecture at Georgetown University. His words ring even more true today: "The problem, in a nutshell, was this: In all of those programs—in education and justice and child welfare and neighborhood improvement—we were trying to reform huge, complex, entrenched, multi-billion-dollar public systems. . . . We were fighting battles that had tested the power and wealth of serial U.S. Congresses and presidencies. It was a battle of Homeric proportions fought with Lilliputian resources."[30] Stanford professor William Damon echoed this sentiment, writing that "foundations simply fail to think through the issues and how to best go about dealing with them. Instead, they get caught up in attractive rhetoric that makes solutions sound much easier than they really are."[31]

For technology entrepreneurs, who have the greatest need for a highly skilled workforce, continuing to invest in a failed system is a waste of resources. The tech world is all about disruptive innovation—and education should be too. Competition and deregulation, the drivers that made the US tech industry the greatest economic force in the world, need to be unleashed on education.

A Different Way Forward for Philanthropy

Philanthropic dollars, used wisely, can have immense power over education. Contributions that have made a difference include those to successful charter school networks, such as KIPP or Success Academies in New York. Additionally, funding scholarships that aid low- to middle-income students seeking to escape their district public schools have increased the opportunity for many. Finally, investments in innovative schools and the technology that enables them, which Gates and Zuckerberg are both exploring, have the potential to greatly impact the lives of teachers and students.

Philanthropists such as Julian Robertson have chosen to back charter networks with proven track records; gifts such as his $25 million to Success Academy incentivized the creation of new schools.[32] Similarly, the Walton Family Foundation announced the investment of more than $100 million to "support diverse and innovative school models and leaders." Their grant beneficiaries are "proven organizations, like those that help create successful charter schools, with an expanded focus on innovative school models." They also back the Partnership Schools in New York, which seek to bring a proven turnaround model to struggling Catholic schools.[33] These investments are successful because they help support individuals and nonprofits who are already inspiring meaningful change in education. Additionally, unlike some donations, they do not come with mandates or additional red tape. They simply enable the organizations to do more of what they are already doing well: educating children.

Other foundations prefer to invest directly in scholarship programs, which is especially beneficial in states that have yet to pass school choice programs. Notably, the Schwarzman family gave the substantial sum of $40 million in 2015 to the Inner-City Scholarship Fund, an organization that provides tuition assistance to low-income children attending Catholic schools in the archdiocese of New York. The fund supports more than seven thousand students attending Catholic schools, 92 percent of whom are minorities. An impressive 98 percent of Inner-City Scholarship Fund recipients graduate from high school, 96 percent of whom pursue higher education. Similarly, New York publisher Ted Forstmann and John Walton cofounded the Children's Scholarship Fund (CSF) to increase access to private and parochial schools for low-income families. Since its founding, CSF has provided scholarships worth $789 million, improving the lives of 174,000 children. The graduation rates and college attainment of these scholarship recipients also far outstrip those of local public schools.[34]

A final investment area of note involves educational technology startups. Philanthropists would do well to invest in more student-centered software research and development. Once this technology is developed, they can also work toward making it available to all types of schools, especially those most in need. Ironically, in Africa, Gates, Zuckerberg, and the World Bank have invested heavily in Bridge International Academies, a chain of innovative, technology-focused private schools that serve disadvantaged children.[35] Yet, in the United States, their giving typically supports variations of the status quo. There is some evidence to suggest that philanthropy is shifting to support more educational technology, but it has not yet impacted American classrooms in the way it could. Simply giving away computers and software does not transform education. Worldwide funding for educational technology reached $9.52 billion in 2017, up 30 percent from 2016, yet pre-K–12 educational technology providers received only 13 percent of the overall global investment.[36]

Foundations seeking to improve education must move away from the empty platitudes of "think big" philanthropy to more meaningful "think small" giving. Senior fellow at the Hudson Institute William Schambra highlights this distinction in an insightful essay, arguing that philanthropies should not try to change a large, complicated problem all at once but rather have the humility to solve many smaller iterations of the broader issue. He agrees that the best way to do this is through supporting local actors who have been chipping away at societal problems for decades with limited resources. Schambra writes,

> Embedded in the most hard-pressed neighborhoods around the country are to be found grassroots groups, launched and sustained by the residents themselves. They are already successfully tackling the most difficult problems they face, reflecting the moral and religious principles most important to them. These groups are virtually invisible to the world of foundations, because they don't have professional fund-raisers or fancy brochures; they don't speak the arcane language of social science but rather the stark and simple language of faith; above all, they don't purport to get to the root causes of poverty, just to care for the poor and to help them, one-by-one, work their way out of their condition.[37]

This approach was exemplified by the Lynde and Harry Bradley Foundation, with which Schambra was previously affiliated. The Bradley Foundation supported grassroots groups in Milwaukee in 1990 to bring about the nation's first school voucher program. It was tiny to start—fewer than one thousand students—but served as the catalyst for transforming not only education in Milwaukee but school choice programs around the country.

Foundations should seek out and fund these "invisible" local groups to truly have an impact, Schambra argues. Additionally, these big-dollar donors must approach the project of education reform with humility; money is not the answer to every issue, and elite experts do not always know what is best for our children and our schools. All of the reforms we advocate are designed to allow those with the greatest hands-on knowledge and skin in the game to have a primary influence over learning.

Overall, investments are more likely to create lasting change if they return educational authority to reputable local actors and empower parents to choose the school that best meets the needs of their child. Dollars given with the strings of federal bureaucracy or complex mandates attached are not attractive even to the neediest schools. Philanthropic organizations would be wise to reward what is already working—certain charter networks, inner-city Catholic schools, and meaningful technology in innovative schools—rather than seeking to impose more tests and standards from state and national governments.

Schools That Work: Ripe Ground for Future Investment

The following schools illustrate the innovative models that philanthropies could fund. This list is by no means exhaustive but rather highlights a few groundbreaking models. Each school challenges the status quo differently; all represent twenty-first-century learning.

Intrinsic Schools: Rewriting the Rules

Longtime Chicago Public Schools (CPS) teachers and administrators Ami Gandhi and Melissa Zaikos are rewriting the rules about schooling. Both initially tried to spark innovation within the behemoth Chicago Public Schools and its six hundred schools. Yet Gandhi and Zaikos each realized that innovation within the district was simply not possible. Too many structural constraints and immovable obstacles existed. To create Intrinsic Schools, they had to circumvent the traditional system.[38]

Walking into Intrinsic immediately confers a sense of purposeful learning and community. This seventh- to twelfth-grade campus in Chicago's Belmont neighborhood takes previously underserved students and propels them to postsecondary success. Intrinsic has earned Chicago Public Schools' highest rating for academic success all while serving high proportions of low-income, minority, and first-generation college students. Ninety-one percent are Latino, 19 percent are classified as having an academic or physical disability, 13 percent are English language learners, and 86 percent qualify for free or reduced-price lunch. The school receives three applications for every open seat; students are admitted randomly via lottery, and there is no academic test for admission (unlike many of Chicago's high-performing, selective-enrollment public schools).[39] Though its students look remarkably like those in the poorest-performing schools in Chicago, Intrinsic could not be more different.

After leaving CPS, Gandhi reported that she and Zaikos went on a listening tour across the nation, visiting a wide variety of innovative schools. Upon returning to Chicago in 2013, they bought an old warehouse building and began a revolution in charter schooling, with Zaikos as CEO and Gandhi as chief learning officer. Intrinsic's charter school employs common learning spaces and shared classes of students, with teachers and support staff working more as teams than as individuals. Classrooms are large open spaces called "pods," which contain as many as sixty students at a time. Though all students within a pod are in the same grade, their experiences look different based on their level and learning needs. Some may be learning precalculus through explanations from a teacher in one corner, another group working on algebra collaboratively with peers and a tutor in another, and others working on a math software program on their laptops at independent workstations lining the walls.

The school days are divided into ninety-minute blocks, with different classes meeting Monday and Thursday from those meeting Tuesday and Friday. For Wednesdays this year, Intrinsic introduced a new schedule based on student feedback. After listening to students, Gandhi reported that most wanted to participate in extracurricular activities while also having time for more tutoring. Yet most students work after school or take care of siblings, rendering them unable to attend clubs or meet with teachers during that time.

Now, though students attend a typical core content course in their first and last block periods on Wednesday, the two blocks in the middle of the day are reserved for extracurricular activity meetings and tutoring. Intrinsic empowers students to seek out the academic resource they need during the tutoring block. Choosing to meet in the math room with older peer tutors, the English room with teachers, or a quiet study space just to catch up on work, students direct their own learning. Research shows that meaningful choice in education is crucial for inspiring intrinsic motivation and learning outcomes; Intrinsic employs this research-based practice in a unique way.[40]

The exact opposite of one-size-fits-all, Intrinsic intentionally differentiates and structures learning experiences with the success of both teachers and students in mind. Gandhi noted that the model explicitly works to reframe the role of teacher. Rather than serving as content creators and planners extraordinaire for 120+ students a day, as in the traditional model, teachers focus on building relationships with students and responding to their needs in real time. Teachers are expected to work in teams, and for that purpose have ninety minutes of team planning time built into their day.

When I visited Intrinsic in Spring 2019, there was a palpable difference in ethos. Observing a group of teachers during their common planning time was absolutely fascinating after working in a school where collaboration between grade- and subject-level teachers happened at best via email and at worst not at all. The teachers bounced ideas off one another, smiling and referencing what had worked well and what more could be done to engage students. A professional strategy session was unfolding before my eyes, harnessing the collective power of a number of passionate, motivated, and kind-hearted adults to better serve their students' needs.

Other strengths of Intrinsic's model include student-led conferences. Rather than being a meeting between parent and teacher, these conferences allow students to present their achievements, strengths, weaknesses, and goals to their parents in the presence of educators. A designated advisory period focused on metacognitive reflection helps students plan these presentations, and the school has witnessed a remarkable 95 percent parent attendance at conferences. Finally, there is an intentional focus on connecting learning to the real world. At each grade level, students complete a capstone project focused on complex, real-world problem solving, and the twelfth-grade year provides ample opportunity for students to pursue apprenticeships and dual-credit enrollment at a local college. "If the twelfth-grade year doesn't look significantly different, we aren't preparing them for postsecondary education," Gandhi said with a smile.

Intrinsic does face one major issue: standardized test day. The issue is not with scores, however. To the contrary, Intrinsic students score well above the average for CPS and only slightly below selective-enrollment schools (which only accept students of extremely high academic caliber). The issue is that Intrinsic has no desks. Every space in the school is collaborative; thus, to test students in a spaced-out, row-arranged way requires some heavy furniture lifting. Gandhi quipped that teachers literally spend "hours moving furniture before test day because we still test like it's the 1950s."

State-mandated testing aside, Gandhi is happy with the model and how the school has grown in a way that is responsive to student and community needs. She and Zaikos believe that "the model is never finished": they will continue to innovate so as to give students the best possible education. Despite national praise and local demand (three applications for every seat) for Intrinsic, Chicago Public Schools blocked the model's expansion to a downtown campus.[41] CPS is, ironically, the city's charter authorizer, despite its tense relationship with the charter sector as a whole.[42] Gandhi and Zaikos eventually appealed to the Illinois Board of Education, which authorized them without hesitation.

Cristo Rey: Social Capital and Corporate Responsibility

Cristo Rey—Christ the King in Spanish—pioneered a blend of high school and professional apprenticeships before they were in vogue. Founded in 1996 in Chicago, Cristo Rey intentionally equips low-income youth for postsecondary and career success. Today, the network has grown to thirty-five schools in twenty-two states, serving 98 percent students of color and 12,012 from economically disadvantaged families. Since its inception, Cristo Rey has graduated 15,505 students, and their students are three times more likely than the total US low-income population to *complete* a bachelor's degree.[43]

Though the Catholic school sector faces ongoing funding and enrollment challenges in many states (especially in those without private school choice programs), Cristo Rey continues to expand its network. Cristo Rey's integrated work-study experience sets its model apart from all other schools. Interestingly, students are only in school four days a week. Students spend the final weekday working, for pay, at a professional internship. Through their Corporate Work Study Program, Cristo Rey schools help build a pipeline of diverse, twenty-first-century talent, preparing underserved youth for the demands of the workplace and future economy.[44]

Students are grouped into four-person teams, which combine to make up one entry-level position at a business. Employers are overwhelmingly satisfied: 95 percent of students meet or exceed workplace expectations, and the program has swelled to more than 3,400 nationally recognizable corporate partners.[45] Students hone the important soft skills of timeliness, collaboration, communication, and resourcefulness at their job—all while growing their professional network. Research suggests that low-income students lack social capital: the connections that often help young people get jobs during and after college.[46] Closing not only the academic gap for low-income students of color but also the social capital gap, Cristo Rey is yet another outstanding example of bringing learning into the twenty-first century.

Last, but certainly not least, the faith component of Cristo Rey schools makes them distinctive. The Catholic Church has historically served marginalized communities, and Cristo Rey schools continue to do so today. Providing students with not only an education but an *excellent* education, Cristo Rey's distinctive Catholic character helps students explore religion, faith, and spirituality. Cristo Rey's focus on service to the community is key; students learn to share the gifts of education and training they have been given with the broader world.

High Tech High: An Interdisciplinary Approach

High Tech High (HTH), a charter network in San Diego, California, is all about interdisciplinary and project-based learning. Rather than taking math, English, science, and history, students choose among a much more integrated set of course offerings, such as humanities-Spanish. Students work with teachers to create meaningful, semester-long projects that they present to professionals in a variety of fields.[47]

High Tech High opened in September 2000 and has since expanded into an integrated network of fourteen charter schools serving students in grades K–12. The school's founding principles are equity, personalization, authentic work, and collaborative design.[48] Incorporating integrated subject matter coupled with an integrated school (the schools enroll from a zip code–based lottery), HTH prioritizes equity. Holding all students to high standards, HTH does not track students into advanced, middle, or lower level classes.

A distinctive focus for HTH is its teachers. The network prioritizes hires with interdisciplinary backgrounds, and teachers are given great autonomy over their students and courses. Teachers are encouraged to design courses and projects around real-world themes: each student has to develop an original physical product to represent his or her learning over a semester. Teachers work one-on-one with students to develop a project of interest, design learning tasks, and divide the creation of the project into smaller parts. Rather than teaching subjects in individual chunks and moving on, the learning process is reframed as one that is ongoing, interwoven, and collaborative.

The student projects on HTH's website give insight into their transformational learning model.[49] In a project called "Breaking Bread," twelfth-graders reverse-engineered bread machines (physics), while studying what a group's type of bread tells us about its history and culture (humanities), and using modeling to understand the different nutritional levels within bread during stages of the bread-making process (math and health).[50] In a project called "In Sickness and in Health," eleventh-grade students used art, biology, and the humanities to study personalized medicine in the modern world.[51] They earned a grant through the National Science Foundation to partner with several researchers at University of California–San Diego throughout the project. Finally, even younger students at HTH learn the value of relating subject areas to one another and to the surrounding world. Students in second grade at HTH played the role of scientists to investigate the role of bees in our ecosystem and what will happen if they disappear. After researching, students became artist advocates, creating plays to educate teachers and parents about the role of bees. Finally, students wrote letters to city officials and corporations, in addition to planting more than two hundred bee-friendly plants in a community service project.[52]

Sound like a school of the future? We think it sounds like the schools we need more of today.

Citizen Schools: Employing a Different Type of Teacher

The Boston-based Citizen Schools leverage the power of the community to bring more STEM opportunities to youth historically underrepresented in these fields. Though one-third of the US population is Black or Latino, only 8 percent work in STEM-related fields. Citizen Schools serve more than one hundred thousand students in twenty-eight communities to try to rectify that gap.[53]

Three important features of its model are an expanded classroom focus, an extended day, and community partnerships. Expanding the classroom is the innovative idea that students learn not only from their teachers but also from real-world practitioners. Citizen Schools recruit engineers, researchers, and scientists as volunteers to run hands-on learning experiences for students during the school day. Research shows that students in upper-income families spend three hundred more hours each year engaging with enriching experiences outside of the classroom than do the three million children in lower-income households.[54] By the time these two groups reach middle school, lower-income children run a deficit of nearly six thousand hours of enrichment time. These schools support academic achievement in core subjects such as reading and math, but their main focus is on sparking middle schoolers' curiosity through creativity and hands-on experiences.[55]

Community partnerships plus an expanded classroom ethos result in meaningful apprenticeship opportunities for students. Every semester, all students participate in a ten-week apprenticeship taught by "Citizen Teachers." Students have worked as apprentice lawyers, website designers, financial advisers, robot engineers, and even pilots. Students complete an accompanying unit of study that combines multiple subjects (similar to High Tech High's approach).[56] Though more schools are beginning to encourage professional apprenticeships, few do so at the middle school level. Arguably, this is the time in schooling when students are the most energetic, restless, and inquisitive. Rather than crushing that natural curiosity by asking kids to sit at a desk all day, Citizen Schools give students meaningful learning experiences. They enact the idea that we learn best not by hearing or seeing but by doing.

In thinking about this model and its name, I realized that what is really going on here is a mutual exchange of citizenship. In an age when our society is witnessing the fragmentation of communities and decline of traditional institutions such as church and family, models such as this could be an interesting remedy. It's a beautiful thing when adults, well established in their careers or retired, donate their time and expertise to the next generation. Students witness an example of good citizenship while being taught by their citizen teachers.

P-TECH: A Public-Private Partnership

Pathways in Technology Early College High Schools (or P-TECH for short) are distinct from all other school types because they are the brainchild of a Fortune 500 company: IBM.[57] In recent years, IBM found that too few college graduates have the requisite skills to succeed in the twenty-first-century workplace. Rather than waiting for schools to change what they teach, IBM simply launched its own school in 2011. Since then, the P-TECH model has expanded rapidly to more than one hundred schools in four countries. P-TECH's students, who are predominantly minority and low income, earn a high school diploma and an industry-recognized associate's degree, and benefit from relevant work experience in a STEM-related field during the six-year program.[58] In an age when career and technical programs for high schools often do not align with workforce demands, P-TECH leverages the power of partnerships in a rather obvious way to break down the silos dividing public higher education, private industries, and schools.[59]

P-TECH fundamentally restructures traditional patterns of enrollment, coursework, and postsecondary pathways. Its main mission is to "align and strengthen the relationship between school and work," recognizing the massive mismatch between what American businesses want and what students are learning. Though located in public school districts, P-TECH leaders have autonomy to create curriculum and pathways based on local industry needs— autonomy the rest of the public school system does not enjoy. P-TECH relies on the partnership of three entities in each location to create curriculum for its students: an individual school leader, an industry partner or partners, and a community college partner. All three participate in a skills-mapping process that explores and defines the specific technical, academic, and professional skills required by entry-level jobs. Once identified, the school leader, community college, and industry partners work to detail and backward-map the skills into a six-year curriculum for students. Industry partners also provide professional internships to P-TECH students throughout the six years and commit to prioritizing P-TECH graduates for available entry-level positions.[60]

P-TECH students have numerous advantages upon leaving the program. Some can go directly into careers with the cost-free, STEM-focused associate's degree they earned in the six-year program. Others choose to enroll in a four-year bachelor's program. Most important, students have begun to build a network within an industry of their choice; these mentors will help them after their time at P-TECH ends.[61]

Khan Lab School

Khan Lab School, of Mountain View, California, has a similar focus on personalization and real-world learning. Informed by Salman Khan's "One World Schoolhouse" philosophy, it provides an extended-year, extended-day, mixed-age program with project-based learning.[62] After its first school opened its doors in 2014, Khan also debuted a Khan Lab high school for the 2017–18 school year. Students attend school 8:30 a.m.–6 p.m. throughout the year, with multiweek breaks dispersed through the year.

Khan Lab School, for children ages five to sixteen and over, is one of the first schools to break the silos of grade levels grouped by age. Instead, Khan Lab groups students by level of independence and academic ability. Students are promoted to the next group (not grade) when they have demonstrated mastery of the material and a level of independence, as assessed by teachers.[63] Students here are motivated to take ownership of their learning, as they work with advisers to set their own goals and weekly schedules. Rather than dividing the school day into subjects, students have parcels of time for self-paced work (Ownership Time), small group seminars, and project-based learning (Studio Time). Khan Lab School teaches students content but also the soft skills of time management and productivity; if students' ownership time is used effectively, they are not given homework.[64]

The Khan Lab high school, similar to Intrinsic schools in this way, focuses on space redesign and learning redefinition. A guiding motto is "Everyone's a teacher. Everyone's a student." And school spaces reflect that understanding of learning as a cooperative partnership. Filled with collaborative, technology-rich spaces, as well as places for independent reading and work, the school has "labs" for every subject, where students and faculty are expected to present and display their work. In the Make Lab, students can design, build, and prototype; the Ideate Lab is for brainstorming; and the Chat Lab is for discussing ideas and working through problems. Responsive to change, the design of the school's facility and curriculum reflects that what students learn, and how and where they learn it, will continue to change over time.[65]

Clearly, these schools are rewriting the educational playbook. The innovators who created them recognized the need to circumvent a bureaucratically bound traditional public school system. They are owned and operated by local actors who put the best interests of kids first. Moreover, their different models underscore that education is not a one-size-fits-all endeavor. Students thrive in different settings; providing as many models as possible increases the odds that every student will find a learning environment that motivates him, builds his skills, and gives him options for the future.

Philanthropies should intentionally seek out schools like these when making funding decisions. Empowering local actors to do more of what they are already doing well should be the goal of education philanthropy, not imposing top-down curriculum mandates or throwing more money at a system that fails so many students.

The reforms we advocate would make more schools like these possible. Within the public system, diversity and innovation, fueled by the creativity and imagination of educators, would become the norm, not the exception. And more students would be able to access a plethora of learning experiences outside the system, many of them launched by universities, entrepreneurs, and others whose talents would be gainfully brought to bear in the educational enterprise. Unshackling K–12 education is the key to fulfilling our nation's promise of high-quality education for America's young people.

CHAPTER 9

The Legal Terrain

Law defines the realm of the possible for education reform. All state constitutions guarantee the right to a public education. Reform advocates have deployed those provisions, along with the equal protection clause of the Fourteenth Amendment, to produce changes in K–12 education, many of them profound. Other state constitutional provisions have been wielded to thwart reforms, especially school choice.

Because education is primarily a state and local concern, and the right to an education derives from state constitutions, most of the legal action takes place in state rather than federal courts. As the federal government's role in education has increased, so has federal litigation, mainly over issues surrounding discrimination and children with disabilities. Most disputes over the provision, funding, and organization of public education take place at the state level.

But the federal constitution provides the legal framework within which state provisions operate. Over the past century and more, the US Supreme Court has established four baseline principles that determine in large part what the states must do, what they are permitted to do, and what they may not do. In this chapter, we trace those principles and where they have led.

Parental Liberty

At the turn of the twentieth century, nativism was a powerful political force across America. Much of it was directed toward Catholic immigrants from Ireland and Italy, many of whom brought their schools with them.

Catholic schools were viewed with great hostility by the Ku Klux Klan and other nativists, who sought to enact laws to slow their growth and imperil their existence. One approach involved state constitutional amendments (called Blaine amendments), which were intended to prevent Catholic schools from sharing in public education funding. Another was a more blatant attempt to force all children to attend public schools.

In the 1920s, the US Supreme Court rejected these efforts in several cases establishing that parents, rather than the state, have primary control over their children's upbringing and education. The most famous of these cases was *Pierce v. Society of Sisters* in 1925. The court struck down an Oregon law, supported by the Ku Klux Klan, that required all children to attend government schools. Its ruling, which remains good law today, was emphatic: "The fundamental theory upon which all governments in this Union repose excludes any general power of the State to standardize its children by forcing them to accept instruction from public teachers only," the court declared. "The child is not the mere creature of the State; those who nurture him and direct his destiny have the right, coupled with the high duty, to recognize and prepare him for additional obligations."[1]

The *Pierce* line of cases does not forbid basic state regulation of education, such as compulsory school attendance laws and minimum school curriculum requirements, which private schools also follow. But it has been especially helpful in safeguarding the rights of homeschoolers. As recently as the 1980s, homeschoolers were still being prosecuted for truancy violations.[2] Now homeschooling is legal in all fifty states.

Equal Educational Opportunities

The most seismic event in K–12 education since the creation of the common school was *Brown v. Board of Education*. There the court established a bedrock constitutional principle: education, "where the state has undertaken to provide it, is a right which must be made available to all on equal terms."[3]

Of course, sixty-five years later, we still have a long distance to travel to fulfill that principle. Indeed, the subtitle of this book could well be "Vindicating the Promise of *Brown v. Board of Education*." Our educational problems go beyond inequality, for they afflict nearly everyone. But they are most pronounced among children of modest economic means, especially Black and Hispanic youngsters.

The *Brown* decision was met in many parts of the country, north as well as south, with massive resistance. Troops were brought in to enforce the decision in southern states. For decades, court orders focused on ending both formal and de facto segregation. In many school districts, especially large cities, forced busing and fixed racial ratios were used to eliminate racially identifiable schools. Unfortunately, affluent white families and middle-class Black families fled the school systems and in many instances the cities themselves.[4] Those responses left minority schoolchildren as isolated as ever and eroded the tax base for inner-city school districts.

We cannot accept defeat in fulfilling the promise of *Brown v. Board of Education.* The reforms we advocate will do much to eliminate educational inequality. Eradicating school district lines and school assignments by zip code, and instead allowing open public school enrollment, would greatly alleviate the inequality that is a perpetual feature of American public education. The bottom line, however, is to provide high-quality educational options to all students. The prevalence of well-integrated schools within public and private school choice programs suggests that families of all races and incomes will set aside their differences in the pursuit of quality education. The key imperative is to make such opportunities available to those children who do not have them.

Funding Equity

In the 1970s, education activists began to attack funding disparities between poor and wealthy school districts. In 1973, in *San Antonio Independent School District v. Rodriguez,* a five-to-four majority of the US Supreme Court rejected a claim that a property-based school tax that created funding disparities violated the equal protection guarantee of the Fourteenth Amendment. The court held that the US Constitution confers no fundamental right to education.[5] Although advocates continue to pursue similar claims in federal courts,[6] they have found much greater success in state courts by litigating state constitutional provisions, which may be interpreted to provide greater rights than their federal counterpart and certainly not fewer.

The earliest successful funding equity lawsuits were in New Jersey, under the state constitution's guarantee of a "thorough and efficient education," and California, where the courts recognized a fundamental right to education under the state constitution. Fifty years into court control over education funding, New Jersey spends about $24,000 per student in the Newark Public Schools and more than $28,000 in Camden.[7] Although funding disparity lawsuits designed to achieve educational adequacy and equity have succeeded in more than half the states, leading in many instances to significant funding increases, they have not narrowed the racial and socioeconomic academic gap, as we explained in chapter 2.[8] Indeed, the Supreme Court has observed that the weight of research shows that structural, curricular, and accountability-based reforms, "much more than court-imposed funding mandates, lead to improved educational opportunities."[9]

More recently, advocates such as the American Civil Liberties Union have challenged systemic barriers to equal opportunity in public schools.[10] The exemplar case so far has been *Vergara v. State of California*, in which minority schoolchildren challenged teacher tenure, dismissal, and retention statutes they alleged subjected them to grossly ineffective teachers. Following trial, the superior court enjoined the statutes, but the court of appeal overturned the decision. The California Supreme Court declined to review the decision, over dissenting opinions by Justices Goodwin Liu and Mariano-Florentino Cuéllar. Justice Cuéllar wrote that the case presented "staggering failures that threaten to turn the right to education for California schoolchildren into an empty promise."[11]

So long as unequal educational opportunities persist, creative advocates across the philosophical spectrum surely will continue to argue that essential constitutional guarantees are unfulfilled.

School Choice

Constitutional provisions can be used to limit as well as secure educational opportunities. Ever since the Milwaukee Parental Choice Program was adopted in 1990, legal challenges have followed the adoption of every parental choice program encompassing private schools, and sometimes charter schools as well.

Once religious schools were included among the choices made available to parents, many legal challenges focused on the First Amendment, which forbids governmental establishment of religion. Over the years, the US Supreme Court has expanded the scope of the establishment clause beyond its text.

In the 1970s, a number of states, including New York and Pennsylvania, took steps to mitigate the decline of Catholic schools through various efforts dubbed "parochiaid," which directed support to Catholic schools and families who patronized them. Such efforts were struck down by the Supreme Court in the 1973 decision in *Committee for Public Education v. Nyquist*. This decision seemed to doom subsequent efforts to assist families in using public funds in religious schools. But a footnote in *Nyquist* seemed to hold out hope, suggesting that the court was leaving open the question of "some form of public assistance (e.g., scholarships) made available generally without regard to the sectarian-nonsectarian, or public-nonpublic nature of the institution benefitted."[12]

The Milwaukee program and others that followed were designed to fit within this footnote. Legal challenges ensued under both the establishment clause and state constitutional provisions.[13] After twelve years of non-stop battles, the issue of religious establishment reached the Supreme Court in *Zelman v. Simmons-Harris*, which challenged the constitutionality of Cleveland's voucher program. Designed to assist low-income children in a disastrously bad public system, Cleveland's program allowed families to use public funds to pay for private or suburban public schools (unfortunately, no suburban public schools agreed to participate in the program).

The Supreme Court upheld the program by a five-to-four vote, concluding that the program was neutral regarding religion, as it provided only "indirect aid" in the form of financial assistance to families. The court characterized the program as one of "true private choice," in which families could choose among a number of options.[14] The dissenters, in contrast, predicted that the program would foment "religiously based social conflict."[15] Although school choice programs continue to engender disagreement, they have not produced the religious strife feared by the *Zelman* dissenters. Instead, they have provided educational opportunities to hundreds of thousands of children.

Although *Zelman* removed the federal constitutional cloud that hovered for decades over school choice, it did not end the legal challenges. Robert Chanin, former general counsel for the National Education Association, correctly observed that even if the antichoice advocates lost *Zelman*, they still had an entire legal "toolbox" with which to challenge choice programs.[16] The Florida Supreme Court, for instance, invalidated a voucher program under a state constitutional provision that provides for a "uniform" public education, and the Colorado Supreme Court struck down a voucher program on the grounds that it violated a provision that guarantees local control over education.[17] More recently, after protracted litigation, the Nevada Supreme Court ruled that without an independent basis of funding, the state's ESA program is "without an appropriation to support its operation." In other words, the legislature must figure out how to fund the program through an independent source, or the program is effectively dead.[18]

But the main source of legal concern for school choice advocates involved the so-called Blaine amendments, which are provisions in thirty-eight state constitutions that generally prohibit aid, support, or funding for "sectarian" schools. The state constitutional provisions were promoted by anti-Catholic nativists after they failed, in an effort led by then senator James G. Blaine, to add a similar provision to the US Constitution. Although the term *sectarian* is now understood to equate with *religious*, at the time the amendments were adopted (mostly in the late 1800s), the term was understood to mean Catholic. As Justice Samuel Alito recently explained, state Blaine amendments were "prompted by virulent prejudice against immigrants."[19] School choice proponents argued, sometimes with success, that scholarship programs did not violate the Blaine amendments because they provided aid to students, not schools, but in many states the provisions presented a serious obstacle to school choice programs.

Just a week before we completed this book, the US Supreme Court made the obstacle significantly less onerous in *Espinoza v. Montana Department of Revenue*. Montana adopted a tax-credit scholarship program in which recipients could use scholarships at any private school, religious or secular. The Montana Supreme Court ruled that the program violated its Blaine amendment and invalidated the program.

In a five-to-four decision, in which Chief Justice John Roberts recounted the bigoted history of the Blaine amendments, the court overturned that decision and ruled that the program's exclusion of religious schools and families wishing to send their children to them violates the First Amendment's guarantee of free exercise of religion. The court held that Montana's Blaine amendment, as applied to exclude religious schools from the scholarship program, "discriminates based on religious status."[20] Specifically, "the provision puts families to the choice between sending their children to a religious school" or receiving scholarships.[21]

The court made clear that its decision applies only in specific circumstances: "A State need not subsidize private education. But once a State decides to do so, it cannot disqualify some private schools solely because they are religious."[22] Blaine amendments remain in thirty-eight state constitutions, but by this decision they cannot be used to exclude religious schools from participation in educational benefit programs that include private schools.

A Constitutional Course

Our fifty-one constitutions—one national and fifty state constitutions—reflect the enormous importance Americans attach to educational opportunities. Though the US Constitution does not mention education, its equal protection guarantee eviscerated the separate but equal doctrine and the inherently unequal educational opportunities it produced. And all of our state constitutions affirm the right to an education.

But most of those constitutions were written a long time ago, before the modern challenges and possibilities of public education. Should they prove unequal to the task, citizens who are committed to vindicating the underlying value placed on education can bring about constitutional change. State constitutions are much more easily amended than the US Constitution. One possible amendment would provide that "no provision in the constitution of this state should be construed to limit the ability of the legislature or the people to provide or expand educational opportunities to the children in this State." Other changes could be proposed in various states to effectuate a twenty-first-century public education system.

But even without changes, our existing constitutional guarantees underscore our nation's sacred commitment to education. Our most basic law promises educational opportunities to all. It is up to all of us to make good on that promise.

CHAPTER 10

A Model for Building the Future

Remember the thought experiment from chapter 1? After reading this book, what is the first change you would like to see? Though many of us would likely disagree in our answers to this question, the one consensus that should emerge is that the status quo is unacceptable if our country wishes to further its prosperity, remain globally competitive, and produce an educated citizenry. As entrepreneur Marc Andreessen pointed out in a timely essay during the COVID-19 crisis, now is the time to build. The turmoil brought on by this virus immediately exposed basic structural weaknesses in many of our nation's systems—education among them. Andreessen notes,

> The problem is desire. We need to *want* these things. The problem is inertia. We need to want these things more than we want to prevent these things. The problem is regulatory capture. We need to want new companies to build these things, even if incumbents don't like it, even if only to force the incumbents to build these things. . . . We need to separate the imperative to build these things from ideology and politics. Both sides need to contribute to building.[1]

As we look toward building—in the wake of COVID-19 and a changed constitutional landscape for private school choice—Florida stands out as a national model for reform. Although the Sunshine State has not embraced all the reforms we urge, it has gone farther than any other in pursuing choice and competition coupled with systemic public school reform. And the results are very impressive.

Florida as a National Model

Stephanie Gilbert is a mother of five living in Florida. One hundred and eighty days each year, she drives eighty miles per day, depositing one child at a public school, three more at two different private schools, and finally returning home with her youngest, whom she homeschools. Four of the Gilberts' five children are adopted; each has unique special needs. The Gilberts' children, one of whom has autism and is nonverbal, each require different schooling environments. Without the many options Florida provides, especially the McKay Scholarship for students with special needs, the Gilberts would have been stuck. Thankfully, they are reaping the benefits of Florida's effective educational choice, providing an inspiring example for parents everywhere in the process.[2]

Florida's weather, beaches, and low taxes are not the only benefits to residing in this state. The Sunshine State boasts the nation's most comprehensive approach to education reform. Researcher Matthew Ladner and then governor Jeb Bush dubbed it "the Florida cocktail," because the reforms are multifaceted and widespread. Between 1999 and 2007, Governor Bush implemented an intensive mix of accountability and choice reforms. Leaders following his time in office continue to do so today. Prior to Governor Bush's intervention, Florida was rated one of the worst public education systems in the nation; at one point more than half of the state's fourth-graders didn't qualify as even basic readers on the NAEP.

To remedy these disturbing findings, Bush supported the creation of a tax-credit scholarship program, implemented accountability through grading of schools, incentivized the charter sector, encouraged teachers to get their students to take and pass AP exams, supported virtual schools, and more. Bush's reform program truly targeted all involved in schooling: private schools, district public schools, and charter schools. Other states can learn from Florida's successes in expanding educational opportunity.

Families like the Gilberts certainly have benefited. "I don't know how we could have adopted all these kids with special needs if public schools were our only option," Stephanie told *RedefinED*.[3] Florida's reforms are successful because they provide parents with true educational freedom: the ability to choose the best learning environment for each of their children.

Public School Reforms

Florida's reforms have been successful largely due to their multifaceted approach. Accountability and improvement of the state's district public schools were high on the list. Governor Bush implemented a research-based, transparent system for grading schools in 1999. He wrote, "An analysis of the eight states with multiple years of implementation of the A–F grading system found they were making faster improvements on NAEP 4th and 8th grade reading and math tests than the nation as a whole."[4]

Though school grading was a step in the right direction, a 2015 media exposé describing "failure factories" in Pinellas County rocked the state. When the Pinellas County schools were given an F, state and district leaders sought to fix the problem through myriad approaches. Bush wrote, "An 'F' is not a punishment. It is a distress signal. States and districts can respond with any number of strategies, including more resources, instructional coaches, a change in leadership, and more effective teachers."[5]

In a series of articles, the *Tampa Bay Times* described dismal academic records, resegregation as whiter, richer families fled the area, and extraordinarily high teacher turnover.[6] Specifically, 95 percent of Black students tested in the Pinellas County schools were failing reading or math in 2015, teacher turnover could result in as many as a dozen instructors for one class in a single year, and students reported feeling unsafe when attending school.[7]

Those implementing the grading system for schools were careful to make clear that the grading scale was not intended to stigmatize failing schools but rather to help them improve. An exhaustive five-year study found that schools receiving a grade of F improved test scores the following year and that these improvements "remained for the long term." More important, these schools also engaged in the "significant" policy changes necessary for improvement, such as hiring a strong school leader.[8]

School grades were only one piece of the state's public school reforms. Florida also instituted merit-based incentives for teachers whose students score well on AP exams. Teachers receive a $50 bonus for every student they instruct who passes an AP exam.[9] Additionally, Florida's new governor, Ron DeSantis—a Republican and a staunch supporter of the state's school choice programs—pushed for pay raises for public school teachers, indicating that he intends to continue the work Governor Bush started to improve all schools.[10]

Parents Empowered to Choose

Florida is on pace to be the first state where half of its school-age children exercise school choice. In 2018, 1.7 million students in grades pre-K through twelve attended a school of choice—46.4 percent of the 3.7 million school-age children in the state. They were able to do so using the state's various mechanisms of choice: Florida Tax Credit (FTC) scholarships, Gardiner Scholarships, McKay Scholarships, magnet programs, open-enrollment public schools, charter schools, private schools, homeschools, and full-time virtual instruction.[11] Florida's leaders have committed themselves year after year to incentivizing and expanding school choice programs so that every child has access to an education that fits his or her needs.

 In the early years of Jeb Bush's reforms, choice and accountability worked together: students in any school receiving an F grade for two years in a row received vouchers to leave for private schools if they wished. The first year, only four schools qualified, but dozens more had one F. Every single one of them improved and earned a higher grade the following year. After my then-colleagues and I filed public records requests, we learned that the possibility of kids being able to leave with vouchers helped motivate the schools to improve. The voucher program was struck down by the Florida Supreme Court, so competitive pressures are now more indirect.

Incentivizing the Charter Sector

Florida's legislators, backed by supportive governors, have passed numerous bills to incentivize charter school creation. Since 1996, the number of charter schools in Florida has grown to more than 655 in 2017–18. Enrollment in these publicly funded and privately managed schools tops 295,000 students.

Charter schools in Florida have become increasingly diverse, with a current distribution of 42.3 percent Hispanic students, 20 percent African American students, 31.6 percent white students, and 6 percent students identifying as another race.[12] In 2017, former governor Rick Scott signed into law a $419 million education bill that promoted charter school expansion in the state.[13] Similarly, Governor Ron DeSantis has advocated for charter schools to be funded equitably with district schools.[14]

Florida House Speaker Richard Corcoran enacted a $140 million Schools of Hope program in 2017. This subsidizes charter schools that set up shop in low-income neighborhoods with perpetually failing district public schools. The State Board of Education does not allow just any schools to open in these areas; instead, they select "hope operators" intentionally. By rigorously vetting incoming Hope charters, the state ensures that previously underserved students now have access to the best schools. The four designated hope operators in Florida, all of whom have impressive track records, are Democracy Prep Public Schools, IDEA Public Schools, KIPP, and Somerset Academy.[15]

Schools must meet or exceed the district and state average achievement, the average college attendance rate must exceed 80 percent, the percentage of low-income students at currently operated schools must exceed 70 percent, the operator's audited financial statements must be free of issues, and they must meet other criteria as determined by the State Board of Education.[16] Governor DeSantis continued funding the Schools of Hope program with $40 million in 2019 after IDEA and KIPP confirmed they would open twenty-five schools in Tampa Bay and Miami-Dade, respectively.[17]

Expanding Private School Choice: The Florida Tax Credit Scholarship

Founded in 2001, the Florida Tax Credit (FTC) Scholarship awards scholarships worth up to $6,519 for students in grades K–5, $6,815 for students in grades 6–8, and $7,111 for students in grades 9–12. In total, the program gives more than 106,000 low-income students the choice to consider whether a private school may be a better fit than their zoned public school. The average household income of FTC students' families is $25,749, and 54 percent of the children live with only one parent. Thirty-eight percent of FTC students are

Hispanic, 30 percent are Black, 26 percent are white, and 3 percent are multiracial.[18] They are funded by corporate and insurance premium tax contributions for which donors receive a tax credit.

The range of participating schools is as diverse as the student population. Nearly 1,800 private schools of all sizes and sects throughout the state enroll scholarship students. From the seven-student Walden Middle School in Gulfport to the 1,807-student St. Thomas Aquinas High School in Fort Lauderdale, all see the benefit of accepting students who previously could not afford to attend their school. The typical participating school is small (with an average of 135 students), serves elementary students (37 percent of recipients are in K–2, and 63 percent are in grades K–5), and is faith based (69 percent).[19]

Nuts and Bolts

It is worth digging into some of the nuts and bolts that make the Florida Tax Credit Scholarship the most successful program of its kind. Tax-credit scholarships incentivize individuals and businesses to donate private funds to nonprofit organizations that provide scholarships. These nonprofits (also called Scholarship Granting Organizations, or SGOs) then administer the scholarship application and granting process for qualifying students. Florida's main SGO is called Step Up for Students.

In Florida, businesses receive a dollar-for-dollar tax credit for contributions to an SGO. The credit can be applied to the corporate income tax, insurance premium tax, oil and gas tax, alcoholic beverage tax, and more. Contributions are capped each year: the cap for 2018–19 was $873 million. The cap increases by 25 percent when 90 percent of the donation cap was met the previous year. Thus, the program will likely continue to expand, provided that demand continues to increase as well.[20]

Florida's model works well due to its streamlined scholarship granting process. Step Up for Students collects scholarship applications and processes them efficiently through the same system, minimizing the risk that applications fall through the cracks or that the neediest are not served first. SGOs—like any good nonprofit—must have both autonomy and clarity about their mission in order to serve others.[21] They also simplify what can be a complicated process for parents (especially those for whom English is not the first language).

Short-Term Success

Short-term success stories from Florida's reforms abound. In 2017, Florida was the only state in the nation to improve on *both* fourth- and eighth-grade math and reading on the 2017 NAEP.[22] Its gains in math and science persisted on the 2019 NAEP as well.[23] Most notably, Florida has made more progress than any other state on closing racial and socioeconomic achievement gaps. In 2017, the state found that poor and minority students score better on state standardized tests when enrolled in charter schools. While the overall reading test pass rate for high school charter students was six percentage points higher than for students at district schools, it was ten percentage points higher for low-income students, twelve points higher for Hispanic students, and four points higher for Black students. The achievement gap between white and minority students was also smaller among charter school students.[24]

Beyond test scores, parents overwhelmingly report satisfaction with the program. A study of more than fourteen thousand Florida parents and guardians found that 89 percent of parents were "completely satisfied" with the scholarship program. Eighty-three percent were "completely satisfied," and 10 percent were "somewhat satisfied" with their school options. When asked why parents chose a certain school for their scholarship, 66 percent ranked "religious environment/instruction" as important, 52 percent ranked "morals/character values instruction," and 36 percent ranked "safe environment." Moreover, parents overwhelmingly reported that their students were doing well in their schools of choice.[25] As the primary educators of their children, parental opinion should always be considered an important metric of short-term success—and parental satisfaction among choice parents in Florida is off the charts compared with low-income families with children in public schools nationwide.

Additionally, the state has strong accountability measures for all schools of choice. Florida has been strong in closing charter schools that do not meet ethical standards. A common critique of this sector is that it lacks the oversight of traditional public schools. Unfortunately, there have been a few incidents in which bad actors opened schools. Yet the state has swiftly countered these incidents. For instance, Marcus May, the former owner of Newpoint Education Partners, is currently serving a twenty-year sentence and facing a $5 million fine for two counts of racketeering and one count of organized fraud. As CEO of a charter management company, May filled his own pockets through a money-laundering scheme. Florida officials closed or placed under new management all of his company's schools.[26]

Indeed, poorly performing charter schools actually have *more* oversight than traditional district schools. They experience two layers of accountability: the state and parents. Parents can pull their children out of schools of choice they sense are mismanaged or academically lacking. This heightened scrutiny on the charter sector has led to improved outcomes for children. Sixty-eight percent of charter schools earned an A or B grade in 2018, and only 6 percent earned a D or an F.[27]

Long-Term Success

Florida has also steadily reduced long-term achievement gaps since 2012, including the statewide graduation rate and college-degree attainment.[28]

A 2017 study of the Florida Tax Credit Scholarship by the Urban Institute found that students who participate are more likely to enroll in a public college in Florida, as compared with similarly disadvantaged students in public schools. Participation increased enrollment rates by 15 percent overall and by 43 percent for students in the program for four or more years.[29] The same researchers updated the study in 2019 to include scholarship recipients attending college somewhere other than Florida. They found that FTC participants were more likely than similar nonparticipants to enroll in both two-year and four-year colleges (both public and private).[30] Twenty-six percent of scholarship recipients did not attend public college in Florida, so the institute's previous study did not include these students in their findings. Moreover, students showed a 12 percent increase in college enrollment if they entered the Tax Credit Scholarship Program in elementary or middle school and a 19 percent increase in college enrollment if they entered it in high school. The study found especially large effects at four-year private nonprofit colleges—the sector most likely to propel students into gainful employment within four years. The FTC rate for those schools was double that of the comparison group.

The size of these effects increases with the length of time students spend in the program. For example, high schoolers who stayed in the voucher program for at least three years "were about 5 percentage points more likely to earn a bachelor's degree, a 50 percent increase."[31]

Shuffling Voting Coalitions

School choice in Florida is also reflected in the state's political landscape. Republican Ron DeSantis won the governorship of Florida in 2018 running on a pro-FTC platform. DeSantis's victory was partially due to a massive voting block shift: he captured 14 percent of the African American vote and 44 percent of the Latino vote. He won double the Black female votes compared to his predecessor, Ron Scott (9 percent), and more than double the GOP's national average among Black women (7 percent), despite running against a Black candidate. In an election decided by fewer than forty thousand votes, this party shift among Black women—the "school choice effect"—proved pivotal.[32]

This demographic shift was unprecedented and unpredicted, as DeSantis was running against the Black Democratic candidate Andrew Gillum. Gillum helped make school choice an issue by campaigning against charter schools and the Florida Tax Credit Scholarship. His education platform included support only for Florida's district public schools, a message that missed the mark among key constituencies. He said on the campaign trail that "we weaken that promise [of high quality, accessible, public education] every time we divert taxpayer funds into private and religious education that benefits some students, but not all."[33] What Gillum failed to recognize is that the low-income FTC participants—70 percent of whom are minority students—are now able to attend schools that were otherwise unavailable to them because of their family's poverty.

Florida's K–12 school system is far from perfect. But the state has done more than any other to bridge the academic gap and expand educational opportunities for children who desperately need them. Florida has demonstrated what can happen when public school reform is paired with choice: students both inside and outside public schools thrive.

Looking Forward

When you drill down to how our nation's school system is constructed in the twenty-first century, you are left feeling puzzled. Why are students in a school building from 7 a.m. to 3 p.m., when research suggests the teen brain is not fully awake until 9 or 10 a.m.? Why are children grouped into levels by their age rather than their ability? Why is school composed of twelve grades when children in other nations are encouraged to pursue professional apprenticeships after tenth grade?[34] Why is our school calendar designed so that children can work on the family farm over the summer when this is no longer the practice of the vast majority of Americans? Why are children taught the same subjects (in largely the same manner) as in the early 1900s despite a massive change in our economy and society? Why is education largely more about credentialing than learning modern, applicable skills? There are no easy answers for these questions other than "that's the way it's always been." We think this answer is unacceptable.

Though education is poised for a giant transformation, reform is a slow, painful process. Often when we take two steps forward, we're also taking one step back. The status quo has extremely powerful defenders, and fear of change is their most potent weapon. Moreover, an issue unique to education reform is that reformers tend to be young and transient; few stay within the sector for the entirety of their career.[35]

A possible reason that few remain in the reform movement could be the stagnation within the sector itself. When policy people or well-intentioned philanthropists arrive with new, innovative ideas, they are met by extraordinarily powerful special-interest groups and a whole lot of red tape. Worse, many teachers regard reformers with great cynicism (and vice versa). In the words of Atticus Finch, "You never really understand a person until you consider things from his point of view . . . until you climb into his skin and walk around in it."[36] Teachers tend to feel that reforms are imposed on them from above, while reformers get frustrated when teachers do not or cannot implement their proposed changes.

Moreover, reforms that attempt to improve education in one fell swoop are destined to fail. No Child Left Behind and Common Core are two examples of this misguided approach. Above all, we should not feel as though schooling in North Dakota need look anything remotely like schooling in New York City. There is no policy that could possibly be the best fit or fix for such massively different geographic areas and populations. Reform should be a fundamentally local affair; grassroots actors are far better equipped to develop proposals for meaningful, lasting change than bureaucrats thousands of miles away.

When reformers encounter an immovable object, they should go around it. Efforts to increase educational freedom through parental choice, charter schools, and homeschooling are witnessing great success, despite what the media would have us believe.[37] These dynamic, positive movements illustrate that if we build it, families will come. The demand is there; the constraints fall on the supply side. We must ensure—especially with the economic downturn likely after the COVID-19 crisis—that the supply of available schools of choice expands rather than constricts. Indeed, the solvency of our state budgets depends upon it.[38] As more families grow accustomed to choice in every other aspect of their lives and find there are new and better ways to educate their children, they will untether from the status quo and contribute to building a twenty-first-century education system. We do not claim, however, that this book will come close to predicting all of the change that will occur if the system is truly unshackled. We have never had an education system designed to change with the times.

Despite all of its reform challenges, education is important to just about every American citizen. For all of our differences and divisions, *we have all experienced K–12 education in some form.* Though you would never know it from the debates, education is the policy issue that unites us. The average person still remembers the name of at least one teacher, whether it be someone who sparked their interest in history, who made them fall in love with literature, or who simply made math a bit more interesting through humor. Thus, we must be even more committed to bettering the mechanism that shapes us throughout our most formative years and binds us together as Americans.

When the education system is finally freed, we may one day look back and wonder why we held it hostage for so long.

Notes

Chapter 2

1. Howard Blume, "15,000 L.A. High School Students Are AWOL Online, 40,000 Fail to Check In Daily amid Coronavirus Closures," *Los Angeles Times*, March 30, 2020, https://www.latimes.com/california/story/2020-03-30/coronavirus-los-angeles-schools -15000-high-school-students-absent; Allison Anderson, "COVID-19 Outbreak Highlights Critical Gaps in School Emergency Preparedness," Brookings, March 11, 2020, https:// www.brookings.edu/blog/education-plus-development/2020/03/11/covid-19-outbreak -highlights-critical-gaps-in-school-emergency-preparedness.

2. Matthew Ladner, "Should We Feel Optimistic or Pessimistic about American K–12 Education's Future?" *RedefinED*, October 14, 2019, https://www.redefinedonline.org/2019 /10/should-we-feel-optimistic-or-pessimistic-about-american-K–12-educations-future.

3. Drew DeSilver, "U.S. Students' Academic Achievement Still Lags That of Their Peers in Many Other Countries," Pew Research, February 15, 2017, http://www .pewresearch.org/fact-tank/2017/02/15/u-s-students-internationally-math-science.

4. "Frustration in the Schools," PDK Poll 2019 of the Public's Attitudes toward the Public Schools, Phi Delta Kappan, September 2019, https://www.pdkpoll.org/results.

5. Ladner, "Should We Feel Optimistic?"

6. "Frustration in the Schools."

7. Andreas Schleicher, *World Class: How to Build a 21st-Century School System* (Paris: Organisation for Economic Cooperation and Development, 2018), 39.

8. Schleicher, *World Class*, 19.

9. Lauren Camera, "NAEP Scores Show Little to No Gains in Math, Reading for U.S. Students," *U.S. News & World Report*, April 10, 2018, https://www.usnews.com/news/best -states/articles/2018-04-10/naep-shows-little-to-no-gains-in-math-reading-for-us-students.

10. DeSilver, "U.S. Students' Academic Achievement Still Lags."

11. Erica L. Green and Dana Goldstein, "DeVos Calls Slump in Reading Scores a 'Student Achievement Crisis,'" *New York Times*, October 31, 2019.

12. Matthew Ladner, "NAEP History, Geography, Civics Scores Paint Dismal Picture," *RedefinED*, April 27, 2020, https://www.redefinedonline.org/2020/04/naep-history -geography-civics-scores-paint-dismal-picture/?fbclid=IwAR2ajx2EvHLc2vQTn6GovTu -bN30QnwEI6s3CzZGoDqHi5bYC_xclH143VI.

13. Andrew J. Coulson, "State Education Trends: Academic Performance over the Past 40 Years," Cato Institute, March 18, 2014, 2.

14. Coulson, "State Education Trends," 54.

15. DeSilver, "U.S. Students' Academic Achievement Still Lags."

16. Schleicher, *World Class*, 42.

17. "Foreign-Born STEM Workers in the United States," American Immigration Council, June 14, 2017, http://www.americanimmigrationcouncil.org/research/foreign -born-stem-workers-united-states.

18. Jeb Bush and Clint Bolick, *Immigration Wars: Forging an American Solution* (New York: Simon and Schuster, 2013), 88–102.

19. "Foreign-Born STEM Workers in the United States."

20. Bush and Bolick, *Immigration Wars*, 91.

21. Jill Barshay, "Inside the Reardon-Hanushek Clash over 50 Years of Achievement Gaps," *Hechinger Report*, May 27, 2019, https://hechingerreport.org/inside-the-reardon -hanushek-clash-over-50-years-of-achievement-gaps.

22. Matthew Ladner, "USA K–12 Achievement Stalled on International Exams," *RedefinED*, December 19, 2019, https://www.redefinedonline.org/2019/12/usa -K–12-achievement-stalled-on-international-exams.

23. Ladner, "USA K–12 Achievement Stalled on International Exams."

24. Walter E. Williams, "Educational Fraud Continues," *Daily Wire*, April 28, 2018, http://www.dailywire.com/news/29989/williams-educational-fraud-continues-walter-e -williams.

25. "The Racial Scoring Gap on the SAT College Entrance Examination," Council of Blacks in Higher Education, November 5, 2018, https://www.jbhe.com/2018/11/the-racial -scoring-gap-on-the-sat-college-entrance-examination.

26. "The Condition of Education: Public High School Graduation Rates," National Center for Education Statistics, updated May 2019, https://nces.ed.gov/programs/coe /indicator_coi.asp.

27. Sarah Butrymowicz, "Struggling Cities and Excelling Suburbs: A Repeated Pattern around the Country," *Hechinger Report*, September 28, 2015, https://hechingerreport.org /struggling-cities-and-excelling-suburbs-a-repeated-pattern-around-the-country.

28. "The Social Experiment," *The Economist*, May 9, 2020, 20.

29. Dana Goldstein, "School Reforms Fail to Lift U.S. on Global Test," *New York Times*, December 3, 2019.

30. Goldstein, "School Reforms Fail to Lift U.S."

31. "Frustration in the Schools."

32. "How We Measure Success," Knowledge Is Power Program (KIPP), accessed April 17, 2020, http://www.kipp.org/results.

33. "Class Struggle," *The Economist*, May 18, 2019, 22–23.

34. Patrick Wall, "In Deal with Union, Newark Agrees to Pay Raises for Teachers with Graduate Degrees," *Chalkbeat*, November 28, 2018, https://chalkbeat.org/posts/newark/2018 /11/28/in-deal-with-union-newark-agrees-to-pay-raises-for-teachers-with-graduate-degrees.

35. John E. Chubb and Terry M. Moe, *Politics, Markets, and America's Schools* (Washington, DC: Brookings, 1990).

36. "Frustration in the Schools."

37. Albert Cheng et al., "Public Support Climbs for Teacher Pay, School Expenditures, Charter Schools, and Universal Vouchers: Results from the 2018 EdNext Poll," *Education Next* 19, no. 1 (Winter 2019): 10, https://www.educationnext.org/public-support -climbs -teacher-pay-school-expenditures-charter-schools-universal-vouchers-2018-ednext -poll.

38. "Frustration in the Schools."

39. Paul DiPerna, Andrew D. Catt, and Michael Shaw, "2019 Schooling in America: Public Opinion on K–12 Education, Busing, Technology, and School Choice," EdChoice, December 2019, https://www.edchoice.org/wp-content/uploads/2019/10 /2019-9-Schooling-in-America-by-Paul-Diperna-Andrew-Catt-and-Michael-Shaw-1 .pdf.

40. Cheng et al., "Public Support Climbs for Teacher Pay."

41. Dominic Rushe, "The US Spends More on Education Than Other Countries; Why Is It Falling Behind?," *The Guardian*, September 7, 2018, https://www.theguardian .com/us-news/2018/sep/07/us-education-spending-finland-south-korea.

42. Schleicher, *World Class*, 48.

43. Coulson, "State Education Trends," 2.

44. Coulson, "State Education Trends," 4.

45. Schleicher, *World Class*, 48.

46. Schleicher, *World Class*, 15.

47. Schleicher, *World Class*, 110.

48. Coulson, "State Education Trends," 57.

49. Schleicher, *World Class*, 205.

50. Schleicher, *World Class*, 15–16.

Chapter 3

1. Dhawal Shah, "Here Are 450 Ivy League Courses You Can Take Online Right Now for Free," Free Code Camp, January 4, 2020, https://www.freecodecamp.org/news/ivy -league-free-online-courses-a0d7ae675869.

2. Matt Barnum, "How Long Does a Big-City Superintendent Last? Longer Than You Might Think," *Chalkbeat*, May 8, 2018, https://www.chalkbeat.org/2018/5/8/21105877/how -long-does-a-big-city-superintendent-last-longer-than-you-might-think.

3. Rick Hess, "Be Wary of Reformers Peddling 'Model' School Districts," *Education Week*, October 15, 2018, https://blogs.edweek.org/edweek/rick_hess_straight_up/2018/10 /be_wary_of_those_reformers_peddling_model_school_districts.html.

4. Benjamin Scafidi, "The School Staffing Surge: Decades of Employment Growth in America's Public Schools," EdChoice, October 2012, 5–6, https://www.edchoice.org /research/the-school-staffing-surge-2.

5. Benjamin Scafidi, "Back to the Staffing Surge: The Great Teacher Salary Stagnation and the Decades-Long Employment Growth in American Public Schools," EdChoice, May 2017, 1, https://www.edchoice.org/wp-content/uploads/2017/06/Back-to-the-Staffing -Surge-by-Ben-Scafidi.pdf.

6. Scafidi, "The School Staffing Surge," 2.

7. Scafidi, "The School Staffing Surge," 16.

8. Scafidi, "Back to the Staffing Surge," 11.

9. Scafidi, "Back to the Staffing Surge," 13.

10. "Class Struggle," 23.

11. Lindsey Burke, "Teacher Strike in Los Angeles Underscores Need for Education Choice," *Daily Signal*, January 16, 2019, http://www.dailysignal.com/2019/01/16/teacher -strike-in-los-angeles-underscores-need-for-education-choice.

12. Scafidi, "Back to the Staffing Surge," 17.

13. Schleicher, *World Class*, 113.

14. Schleicher, *World Class*, 207.

15. This phenomenon was forecast by James Madison, who predicted that the smaller the unit of government, the more easily it would be manipulated by groups seeking to advance their own ends. Federalist no. 10 (Madison), in *The Federalist Papers* (New York: Modern Library, 1937), 60–61.

16. Kevin Carey, "No More School Districts!" *Democracy: A Journal of Ideas*, no. 55 (Winter 2019), https://democracyjournal.org/magazine/no-more-school-districts.

17. Kelly Powell and Ildi Laczko-Kerr, "Are District Attendance Zones Obsolete?," Arizona Charter Schools Association, November 2, 2017, https://azcharters.org/are-district -attendance-zones-obsolete.

18. Scafidi, "Back to the Staffing Surge," 16.

19. Matthew Ladner, "A History of School Districts and the American Caste System," *RedefinED*, December 17, 2019, https://www.redefinedonline.org/2019/12/a-history-of -school-districts-and-the-american-caste-system.

20. Ladner, "A History of School Districts."

Chapter 4

1. "The Condition of Education: Public Charter School Enrollment," National Center for Education Statistics, last updated May 2019, https://nces.ed.gov/programs/coe /indicator_cgb.asp.

2. "The Condition of Education."

3. "The Condition of Education."

4. Jake Logan and Nina Rees, "Here's Proof Parents Like Charter Schools," *Arizona Republic*, September 6, 2019.

5. Corey DeAndelis et al., "Analysis: Charter Schools Yield 53% Greater Return in Investment Than Traditional Public Schools," *The 74*, April 17, 2019, https://www .the74million.org/article/analysis-charter-schools-yield-53-greater-return-on-investment -than-traditional-public-schools.

6. Tim R. Sass et al., "Charter High Schools' Effects on Long-Term Attainment and Earnings," *Journal of Policy Analysis and Management* 35, no. 3 (Summer 2016): 683–706, https://onlinelibrary.wiley.com/doi/abs/10.1002/pam.21913.

7. Rebecca David, "National Charter School Management Overview," Public Charters, August 27, 2018, https://www.publiccharters.org/our-work/publications /national-charter-school-management-overview-2016-17.

8. "How We Measure Success."

9. "Our Approach," KIPP, accessed April 20, 2020, https://www.kipp.org/approach.

10. "Mathematica Research on KIPP schools," KIPP, accessed April 20, 2020, https:// www.kipp.org/results/independent-reports/#mathematica-2019-report.

11. Selim Algar, "Success Academy Touts 99 Percent Pass Rate for Algebra Regents Exam," *New York Post*, December 17, 2018, https://nypost.com/2018/12/17/success -academy-touts-99-percent-pass-rate-for-algebra-regents-exam.

12. BASIS Charter Schools, *Outcomes*, 2019–2020 brochure, 2, http://basisschools.org /downloads/outcomes-brochure.pdf.

13. BASIS Charter Schools, "BASIS Curriculum," 2019, http://www.basised.com /academics/curriculum/connections-curriculum.

14. BASIS Charter Schools, "The Basis Documentary," YouTube, June 6, 2018, http:// www.youtube.com/watch?v=oKkoSBneL9Y.

15. BASIS Charter Schools, *Outcomes*, 10.

16. Jay Matthews, "U.S. High School Rankings by State—Most Challenging Schools," *Washington Post*, May 5, 2017, http://www.washingtonpost.com/graphics/local/high -school-challenge-2017.

17. BASIS Charter Schools, *Outcomes*, 16.

18. BASIS Charter Schools, "Grades 8–12 Curriculum," 2019, http://www.basised.com /academics/curriculum/grades-8-12-curriculum.

19. BASIS Phoenix, "Senior Projects," 2018, http://www.basised.com/phoenix /academics/senior-projects.

20. Maureen Sullivan, "What Are BASIS Charter Schools and How Are They Rewriting the Education Rules?," *Forbes*, January 4, 2017, http://www.forbes.com/sites /maureensullivan/2016/05/23/what-are-basis-charter-schools-and-how-did-they-rewrite -the-education-rules/#4803975ff9ca.

21. BASIS Charter Schools, "The BASIS Documentary."

22. Valerie Strauss, "What the Public Isn't Told about High-Performing Charter Schools in Arizona," *Washington Post*, March 30, 2017, http://www.washingtonpost.com /news/answer-sheet/wp/2017/03/30/what-the-public-doesnt-know-about-high-performing -charter-schools-in-arizona/?utm_term=.b461cb4af922.

23. Craig Harris, "New Orleans Is the First City to Have an All-Charter School System: Can It Work Elsewhere?," *Arizona Republic*, November 29, 2019, https://www .azcentral.com/story/news/local/arizona-investigations/2019/11/25/new-orleans-public -education-goes-all-charter-school-system/2423191001.

24. Harris, "New Orleans Is the First City."

25. Harris, "New Orleans Is the First City."

26. Richard D. Kahlenberg and Halley Potter, "Restoring Shanker's Vision for Charter Schools," American Federation of Teachers, accessed April 20, 2020, https://www.aft.org/ae/winter2014-2015/kahlenberg_potter.

27. Paul Peterson and Albert Cheng, "Exclusive Analysis: New Harvard Study Shows Public Support for Charter Schools Has Jumped 10 Points in Last Year," *The 74*, May 27, 2018, https://www.the74million.org/article/harvard-poll-charter-support-10-points.

28. Erica L. Green and Eliza Shapiro, "Minority Voters Chafe as Democratic Candidates Abandon Charter Schools," *New York Times*, November 27, 2019, https://www.nytimes.com/2019/11/26/nyregion/charter-schools-democrats.html.

29. Lauren Camera, "Poll: Democratic Primary Voters Support Charter Schools," *U.S. News & World Report*, October 7, 2019, https://www.usnews.com/news/elections/articles/2019-10-07/poll-democratic-primary-voters-support-charter-schools.

30. "Class Struggle," 22–23.

31. Cory Booker, "Stop Being Dogmatic about Public Charter Schools," *New York Times*, November 18, 2019, https://www.nytimes.com/2019/11/18/opinion/cory-booker-public-charter-schools.html.

32. Kahlenberg and Potter, "Restoring Shanker's Vision for Charter Schools"; Talia Milgrom-Elcott, "Unionized Charter Schools: An Unlikely Course Our Democracy Depends On," *Forbes*, May 21, 2019, https://www.forbes.com/sites/taliamilgromelcott/2019/05/21/unionized-charter-schools-an-unlikely-course-our-democracy-depends-on/#55d23f5f1cf1.

33. "Unionized Public Charter Schools, 2016–17," National Alliance of Public Charter Schools, accessed April 20, 2020, https://www.publiccharters.org/our-work/publications/unionized-charter-schools-2016-17.

34. For Kids and Country, accessed April 21, 2020, https://forkidsandcountry.org.

35. "Class Struggle," 23.

36. Jennifer Medina and Dana Goldstein, "Strike Throws Cold Water on City's Embrace of Charter Schools," *New York Times*, January 29, 2019.

37. "Crowding Out K–12 Education," *Wall Street Journal*, April 16, 2018, https://www.wsj.com/articles/crowding-out-K–12-education-1523921017.

38. Matthew Ladner, "Arizona Academics Are Better Than You Think and the Best Is Yet to Come," Arizona Charter Schools Association, March 5, 2020, https://azcharters.org/arizona-academics-are-better-than-you-think-and-the-best-is-yet-to-come.

Chapter 5

1. Nicol Turner Lee, "How Parking a Wireless School Bus Can Help Students Get Back to School," *The Hill*, March 30, 2020, https://thehill.com/opinion/education/490174-how-parking-a-wireless-school-bus-can-help-all-students-get-back-to-school.

2. Robin Lake and Bree Dusseault, "A Month In, Districts and Charter Make Progress on Online Instruction and Monitoring Student Progress, Lag in Grading and Attendance," *The 74*, April 15, 2020, https://www.the74million.org/article/analysis-a-month

-in-districts-and-charters-make-progress-on-online-instruction-and-monitoring-student
-progress-lag-in-grading-and-attendance.

3. Dana Goldstein and Eliza Shapiro, "Online School Demands More of Teachers: Unions Are Pushing Back." *New York Times*, April 21, 2020, http://www.nytimes.com /2020/04/21/us/coronavirus-teachers-unions-school-home.html.

4. Schleicher, *World Class*, 63.

5. Rushe, "The US Spends More on Education."

6. Williams, "Educational Fraud Continues."

7. "Our Impact," Teach for America, May 10, 2020, https://www.teachforamerica.org /what-we-do/impact.

8. "About ACE," Alliance for Catholic Education, May 10, 2020, https://ace.nd.edu /about/the-alliance-for-catholic-education.

9. Cheng et al., "Public Support Climbs for Teacher Pay."

10. Shayanne Gal, Marissa Perino, and Leanna Garfield, "The Best and Worst Countries to Be a Teacher, Based on Salary," *Business Insider*, May 10, 2019, https://www .businessinsider.com/teacher-salaries-by-country-2017-5.

11. Scafidi, "The School Staffing Surge," 2.

12. "Civics 101," *The Economist*, March 2, 2019, 22–23.

13. Chad Alderman, "Why Los Angeles Teachers May Strike," *Education Next*, January 7, 2019, http://www.educationnext.org/context-lausds-potential-teacher-strike.

14. Ted Dabrowski and John Klingner, "11 Things You Need to Know about Chicago Teacher Pensions," Illinois Policy, March 1, 2016, https://www.illinoispolicy.org/11-things -you-need-to-know-about-chicago-teacher-pensions.

15. Joanna Allhands, "Pension Costs Could Erase the Impact of Arizona's Teacher Raises: What Will We Do about It?" *Arizona Republic*, January 7, 2020, https://www .azcentral.com/story/opinion/op-ed/joannaallhands/2020/01/07/pension-costs-could-erase -arizona-teacher-raises-solution/2809177001.

16. Julie Turkewitz and Dana Goldstein, "Denver Teachers' Strike Puts Performance-Based Pay to the Test," *New York Times*, February 11, 2019, https://www.nytimes.com /2019/02/11/us/denver-teacher-strike.html.

17. C. Kirabo Jackson, "The Full Measure of a Teacher: Using Value-Added to Assess Effects on Student Behavior," *Education Next* 19, no. 1 (Winter 2019): 63.

18. Jackson, "The Full Measure of a Teacher," 65.

19. Jackson, "The Full Measure of a Teacher," 66.

20. Jackson, "The Full Measure of a Teacher," 67.

21. Schleicher, *World Class*, 113.

22. Omri Ben-Shahar, "Teacher Certification Makes Public School Education Worse, Not Better," *Forbes*, July 21, 2017, https://www.forbes.com/sites/omribenshahar /2017/07/21/teacher-certification-makes-public-school-education-worse-not-better /#3c454993730f.

23. Jay P. Greene, "Futile Accountability Systems Should Be Abandoned," *Education Next* 17, no. 3 (Summer 2017): 51.

24. See, e.g., Michael Cooper, "Unions Face a Balancing Act in #MeToo Arbitration Cases," *New York Times*, May 18, 2019.

25. Joel Klein, "The Failure of American Schools," *The Atlantic*, June 2011, https://www.theatlantic.com/magazine/archive/2011/06/the-failure-of-american-schools/308497.

26. Klein, "The Failure of American Schools."

27. Klein, "The Failure of American Schools."

28. Klein, "The Failure of American Schools."

29. Janus v. AFSCME, 138 S. Ct. 244 (2018).

30. Cheng et al., "Public Support Climbs for Teacher Pay," 10.

31. Michael Q. McShane and Jason Bedrick, "Warren's Insight on Teacher Pay," *Wall Street Journal*, December 4, 2019, https://www.wsj.com/articles/warrens-insight-on-teacher-pay-11575504939.

32. "Public Education in Both California and Texas Is Poor," *The Economist*, June 20, 2019, https://www.economist.com/special-report/2019/06/20/public-education-in-both-california-and-texas-is-poor.

Chapter 6

1. Milton Friedman, *Capitalism and Freedom* (Chicago: University of Chicago Press, 1962).

2. Samuel Stebbins, "These 25 Cities Are Losing More Residents Than They Are Gaining as Population Declines," *USA Today*, March 21, 2019, http://www.usatoday.com/story/money/economy/2019/03/21/population-decline-us-cities-losing-most-residents/39199277.

3. Emily Badger and Bui Quoctrung, "Detailed Maps Show How Neighborhoods Shape Children for Life," *New York Times*, October 1, 2018, http://www.nytimes.com/2018/10/01/upshot/maps-neighborhoods-shape-child-poverty.html.

4. "Tennessee Launches School Finder Website for Parents," American Federation for Children, March 3, 2020, https://www.federationforchildren.org/afc-tn-launches-school-finder-website-for-parents.

5. Nick Gillespie, "Does School Choice Help Students Learn? All Signs Point to Yes," *Reason*, January 21, 2019, https://reason.com/2019/01/21/does-school-choice-help-students-learn-a.

6. "How Does School Choice Affect Public Schools' Funding and Resources?," EdChoice, accessed April 20, 2020, http://www.edchoice.org/school_choice_faqs/how-does-school-choice-affect-public-schools-funding-and-resources.

7. "Rural Schools," National Education Association, accessed April 20, 2020, https://www.nea.org/home/16358.htm.

8. Arianna Prothero, "The Teachers' Unions Have a Charter School Dilemma," *Education Week*, December 14, 2018, http://www.edweek.org/ew/articles/2018/12/14/the-teachers-unions-have-a-charter-school.html; "1. No Caps," National Alliance for Public Charter Schools, accessed April 20, 2020, http://www.publiccharters.org/our-work/charter-law-database/components/1.

9. Josh Cunningham, "Accountability in Private School Choice Programs," National Conference of State Legislatures, accessed April 20, 2020, http://www.ncsl.org /documents/educ/AccountabilityInPrivateSchoolChoice.pdf.

10. David N. Figlio and Cassandra M. D. Hart, "Competitive Effects of Means-Tested School Vouchers," NBER Working Paper no. 16056, June 2010, http://www.nber.org /papers/w16056.

11. Greg Forster, "A Win-Win Solution: The Empirical Evidence on School Choice," Friedman Foundation, 2016, http://www.edchoice.org/wp-content/uploads/2016/05/A -Win-Win-Solution-The-Empirical-Evidence-on-School-Choice.pdf.

12. David N. Figlio, Cassandra M. D. Hart, and Krzysztof Karbownik, "Effects of Scaling Up Private School Choice Programs on Public School Students," NBER Working Paper no. 26758, February 2020, https://www.nber.org/papers/w26758.pdf.

13. "50-State Comparison: K–12 Funding," Education Commission of the States, accessed August 5, 2019, https://www.ecs.org/50-state-comparison-K–12-funding.

14. "Funding for Florida School Districts 2017–2018," Florida Department of Education, 2017, http://www.fldoe.org/core/fileparse.php/7507/urlt/Fefpdist.pdf.

15. Martin Lueken, "The Tax-Credit Scholarship Audit," EdChoice, October 2016, http://www.edchoice.org/wp-content/uploads/2017/03/Tax-Credit-Scholarship-Audit-by -Martin-F.-Lueken-UPDATED.pdf.

16. Lueken, "The Tax-Credit Scholarship Audit."

17. "Public Charter School Enrollment."

18. "Key Facts about Charter Schools," *In Perspective*, 2018, http://www.in-perspective .org/pages/introduction.

19. Quoted in "Parental Choice and Responsibility," Cato Institute, May 13, 2020, https://www.cato.org/education-wiki/parental-choice-responsibility.

20. Lauren Camera, "American Federation of Teachers President under Fire," *U.S. News & World Report*, July 24, 2017, https://www.usnews.com/news/education -news/articles/2017-07-24/weingarten-under-fire-for-linking-private-school-choice-to -segregation.

21. Richard V. Reeves, Nathan Joo, and Grover J. "Russ" Whitehurst, "How School District Boundaries Can Create More Segregated Schools," Brookings, November 20, 2017, https://www.brookings.edu/blog/social-mobility-memos/2017/11/20/how-school -district-boundaries-can-create-more-segregated-schools.

22. Motoko Rich, Amanda Cox, and Matthew Bloch, "Money, Race and Success: How Your School District Compares," *New York Times*, April 29, 2016, https://www .nytimes.com/interactive/2016/04/29/upshot/money-race-and-success-how-your-school -district-compares.html.

23. Goodwin Liu and William L. Taylor, "School Choice to Achieve Desegregation," *Fordham Law Review* 74, no. 2 (2005), http://www.publiccharters.org/sites/default/files /migrated/wp-content/uploads/2015/04/School-Choice-to-Achieve-Desegregation.pdf.

24. "Racial/Ethnic Integration," in *The 123s of School Choice: What the Research Says about Private School Choice Programs in America* (2019 edition), EdChoice, https://www .edchoice.org/wp-content/uploads/2019/04/123s-of-School-Choice.pdf#page=26.

25. "Fast Facts," Engage by EdChoice, accessed May 28, 2019, https://www.edchoice .org/engage/fast-facts.

26. Kristin Blagg and Matthew M. Chingos. "Who Could Benefit from School Choice? Mapping Access to Public and Private Schools," Brookings, March 30, 2017, http://www.brookings.edu/research/who-could-benefit-from-school-choice-mapping -access-to-public-and-private-schools.

27. The Nevada program is currently inactive, as the state legislature did not fund the program in 2017. The Nevada ESA would have been the first universal ESA—i.e., open to any student—in the nation.

28. "ESA Fast Facts and Statistics," Engage by EdChoice, May 28, 2019, http://www .edchoice.org/resource-hub/fast-facts/#esa-fast-facts.

29. "ESA Fast Facts and Statistics."

30. DiPerna, Catt, and Shaw, "2019 Schooling in America."

31. "School Spending per Pupil Increased by 3.2 Percent," United States Census Bureau, May 21, 2018, http://www.census.gov/newsroom/press-releases/2018/school-spending.html.

32. "School Spending per Pupil Increased by 3.2 Percent."

33. "Salary & Benefits," New York City Public Schools, NYC Department of Educa-tion, 2017, https://teachnyc.net/your-career/salary-and-benefits.

34. Jonathan Butcher, "A Primer on Education Savings Accounts: Giving Every Child the Chance to Succeed," Heritage Foundation, September 15, 2017, http://www.heritage.org /education/report/primer-education-savings-accounts-giving-every-child-the-chance-succeed.

35. Butcher, "A Primer on Education Savings Accounts."

36. AZ Rev. Stat. §15-2401 (2015), https://www.azleg.gov/viewdocument/?docName =http://www.azleg.gov/ars/15/02401.htm.

37. Christian Barnard, "Ballot Measure That Would Have Expanded Arizona's Empowerment Scholarship Program Defeated," Reason, November 17, 2018, http://www .reason.org/commentary/arizona-empowerment-scholarship-ballot-defeated.

38. Butcher, "A Primer on Education Savings Accounts."

39. "Mississippi: Equal Opportunity for Students with Special Needs," EdChoice, 2019, http://www.edchoice.org/school-choice/programs/mississippi-equal-opportunity -for-students-with-special-needs-program; "Tennessee: Individualized Education Account Program," EdChoice, 2019, http://www.edchoice.org/school-choice/programs/tennessee -individualized-education-account-program.

40. "Arizona: Empowerment Scholarship Accounts," EdChoice, 2019, http://www .edchoice.org/school-choice/programs/arizona-empowerment-scholarship-accounts.

41. "Nevada: Education Savings Accounts," EdChoice, 2019, http://www.edchoice.org /school-choice/programs/nevada-education-savings-accounts.

42. "Florida: Gardiner Scholarship Program," EdChoice, 2019, http://www.edchoice .org/school-choice/programs/gardiner-scholarship-program.

43. "North Carolina: Personal Education Savings Accounts," EdChoice, 2019, http:// www.edchoice.org/school-choice/programs/north-carolina-personal-education-savings -accounts.

44. Nat Malkus, Adam Peshek, and Gerard Robinson, *Education Savings Accounts: The New Frontier in School Choice* (New York: Rowman and Littlefield, 2017).

45. "Florida: Gardiner Scholarship Program."

46. "Arizona: Empowerment Scholarship Accounts."

47. Butcher, "A Primer on Education Savings Accounts."

48. "ESA Fast Facts and Statistics."

49. Jonathan Butcher and Jason Bedrick, "Schooling Satisfaction: Arizona Parents' Opinions on Esas," EdChoice, 2013, http://www.edchoice.org/wp-content/uploads/2013 /10/SCHOOLING-SATISFACTION-Arizona-Parents-Opinions-on-Using-Education -Savings-Accounts-NEW.pdf.

50. Andrew D. Catt, Don Soifer, and Michael Shaw, "Nevada K-12 and School Choice Survey," EdChoice, March 2019, https://www.edchoice.org/wp-content/uploads/2019/03 /2019-2-NV-Poll.pdf.

51. Rob O'Dell and Yvette Wingett Sanchez, "Parents Spent $700K in School Voucher Money on Beauty Supplies, Apparel: Attempted Cash Withdrawals," *Arizona Republic*, updated October 30, 2018, http://www.azcentral.com/story/news/politics/arizona/2018/10 /29/misspent-school-voucher-funds-exceed-700-k-little-recovered/1780495002.

52. Matt Beienburg, "Fraud in Arizona's Empowerment Scholarship Accounts? Not So Much," *In Defense of Liberty*, January 22, 2019, http://www.indefenseofliberty. blog/2019/01/22/fraud-in-arizonas-empowerment-scholarship-accounts-not-so-much.

53. Beienburg, "Fraud in Arizona's Empowerment Scholarship Accounts?"

Chapter 7

1. "Disruptive Innovations," Christensen Institute, 2019, http://www .christenseninstitute.org/disruptive-innovations.

2. Selim Algar and Carl Campanile, "Coronavirus-Style Remote Learning Could Replace Old Model Of Education, Cuomo Says," *New York Post*, May 5, 2020, https:// nypost.com/2020/05/05/coronavirus-style-remote-learning-could-be-schools-wave-of -future-cuomo.

3. Algar and Campanile, "Coronavirus-Style Remote Learning."

4. Nellie Bowles, "The Digital Gap between Rich and Poor Kids Is Not What We Expected," *New York Times*, October 26, 2018, http://www.nytimes.com/2018/10/26/style /digital-divide-screens-schools.html.

5. Ruben R. Puentedura, "SAMR: A Brief Intro," in *As We May Teach: Educational Technology, from Theory into Practice* (blog), February 4, 2009, http://hippasus.com /rrpweblog/archives/2015/10/SAMR_ABriefIntro.pdf.

6. Kelly Blair, "Decoding Adaptive," *EdSurge*, 2016, http://d3e7x39d4i7wbe.cloud front.net/static_assets/PearsonDecodingAdaptiveWeb.pdf.

7. Corey DeAngelis, "Why Government-School Monopolists Are Freaking Out," *Washington Examiner*, April 23, 2020, https://www.washingtonexaminer.com/opinion /why-government-school-monopolists-are-freaking-out.

8. Tommy Schultz, "National Poll: 40% of Families More Likely to Homeschool after Lockdowns End," American Federation for Children, May 14, 2020, https://www .federationforchildren.org/national-poll-40-of-families-more-likely-to-homeschool-after -lockdowns-end.

9. Veronique Mintz, "Why I'm Learning More with Distance Learning Than I Do in School," *New York Times*, May 5, 2020, https://www.nytimes.com/2020/05/05/opinion /coronavirus-pandemic-distance-learning.html.

10. DeAngelis, "Why Government-School Monopolists Are Freaking Out."

11. "About K12," K12, May 17, 2020, https://www.k12.com/about-k12.html; "Academic Courses," Primavera, May 17, 2020, https://www.primavera-online-high-school.com /academics/courses.

12. Scott Kent, "Florida Virtual School Likely to Be 'New Normal' in Sunshine State and Beyond," *RedefinED*, May 13, 2020, https://www.redefinedonline.org/2020/05/florida -virtual-school-likely-to-be-new-normal-in-sunshine-state-and-beyond.

13. "A Brief History of Homeschooling," Coalition for Responsible Home Education, October 8, 2018, http://www.responsiblehomeschooling.org/homeschooling-101/a-brief -history-of-homeschooling.

14. Sarah Grady, "A Fresh Look at Homeschooling in the U.S.," National Center for Education Statistics, September 26, 2017, https://nces.ed.gov/blogs/nces/post/a-fresh-look -at-homeschooling-in-the-u-s.

15. Brian D. Ray, "General Facts, Statistics, and Trends," National Home Education Research Institute, March 23, 2020, https://www.nheri.org/research-facts-on -homeschooling.

16. "Homeschool Demographics," Coalition for Responsible Home Education, October 8, 2018, http://www.responsiblehomeschooling.org/homeschooling-101 /homeschool-demographics.

17. "Homeschool Demographics."

18. Melinda D. Anderson, "The Radical Self-Reliance of Black Homeschooling," *The Atlantic*, May 17, 2018, http://www.theatlantic.com/education/archive/2018/05/black -homeschooling/560636.

19. Greg Toppo, "Black Students Nearly 4x as Likely to Be Suspended," *USA Today*, June 7, 2016, http://www.usatoday.com/story/news/2016/06/07/black-students-nearly-4x -likely-suspended/85526458.

20. Ariel Jao, "Segregation, School Funding Inequalities Still Punishing Black, Latino Students," NBCNews, January 12, 2018, https://www.nbcnews.com/news/latino /segregation-school-funding-inequalities-still-punishing-black-latino-students-n837186.

21. Anderson, "The Radical Self-Reliance of Black Homeschooling."

22. "Our Vision," National Black Home Educators, 2014, http:// www.nbhe.net/about -us/our-vision.

23. Monica Olivera, "About Me," *Mommy Maestra* (blog), 2010, http://www .mommymaestra.com/p/about-me.html.

24. Cheryl Fields-Smith, *The Wiley Handbook of Home Education* (West Sussex, UK: John Wiley & Sons, 2017), 213–17.

25. Fields-Smith, *The Wiley Handbook of Home Education.*

26. Jason Tanz, "The Techies Who Are Hacking Education by Homeschooling Their Kids," *Wired,* June 3, 2017, http://www.wired.com/2015/02/silicon-valley-home -schooling.

27. Samantha Matalone Cook, "Making and Child Development: How Making and Hacking Supports Learners," *Samantha Matalone Cook* (blog), February 6, 2017, http:// www.samanthamatalonecook.com/making-and-child-development-how-making-and -hacking-supports-learners.

28. Elizabeth Cook, "'Do-It-Yourself' Home Schooling Growing in Silicon Valley," CBS San Francisco, June 23, 2014, http://www.sanfrancisco.cbslocal.com/2014/06/23/do-it -yourself-home-schooling-growing-in-silicon-valley.

29. Cook, "'Do-It-Yourself' Home Schooling Growing in Silicon Valley."

30. "Academics," Regina Caeli, 2014, http://www.rcahybrid.org/Academics /HybridEducationalApproach.

31. John Holt, *Growing without Schooling: A Record of a Grassroots Movement* (n.p.: Holt Associates, 1997).

32. Jeremy Redford et al., "Homeschooling in the United States: 2012," National Center for Education Statistics, April 2017, http://www.nces.ed.gov/pubs2016/2016096 rev.pdf.

33. Sir Ken Robinson, "Do Schools Kill Creativity?" *TED,* 2006, http://www.ted.com /talks/ken_robinson_says_schools_kill_creativity/up-next?language=en.

34. See, e.g., Pierce, Governor of Oregon, et al. v. Society of the Sisters of the Holy Names of Jesus and Mary, 268 U.S. 510 (1925).

35. Daniel Koretz, *The Testing Charade: Pretending to Make Schools Better* (Chicago: University of Chicago Press, 2019).

36. "Study Reveals How Many Required Tests Students Take," CBS News, October 26, 2015, http://www.cbsnews.com/news/study-reveals-how-many-required-tests -students-take.

37. Kelly Wallace, "Parents 'Opting out' of Standardized Testing," CNN, April 24, 2015, http://www.cnn.com/2015/04/17/living/parents-movement-opt-out-of-testing-feat /index.html.

38. Robinson, "Do Schools Kill Creativity?"

39. Don Batt, "Standardized Tests Are Killing Our Students' Creativity, Desire to Learn," *Denver Post,* April 30, 2016, https://www.denverpost.com/2013/03/07/standardized -tests-are-killing-our-students-creativity-desire-to-learn.

40. Derrick Bryson Taylor, "'Why the Caged Bird' Falls Silent: A School Board Is Cutting Classics," *New York Times,* April 30, 2020.

41. Kate Hardiman, "California Approves Controversial Sex Education Framework for Public Schools," *Washington Examiner,* May 13, 2019, https://www.washingtonexaminer .com/red-alert-politics/california-approves-controversial-sex-education-framework-for -public-schools.

42. Frederick M. Hess, *The Same Thing Over and Over: How School Reformers Get Stuck in Yesterday's Ideas* (Cambridge, MA: Harvard University Press, 2010).

43. David French, "The Trouble with 'Dispositions,'" FIRE, September 21, 2005, http://www.thefire.org/the-trouble-with-dispositions.

44. Adam Kissel, "'Omaha World-Herald' Covers U. Minnesota's Teacher Ed Scandal Regarding 'Cultural Competence' Requirement," FIRE, July 11, 2011, http://www.thefire .org/omaha-world-herald-covers-u-minnesotas-teacher-ed-scandal-regarding-cultural -competence-requirement-2.

45. Brian D. Ray, "African American Homeschool Parents' Motivations for Homeschooling and Their Black Children's Academic Achievement," *Journal of School Choice* 9, no. 1 (March 11, 2015): 71–96, https://www.tandfonline.com/doi/abs/10.1080/15582159.2015 .998966.

46. "Why Colleges Are Recruiting Homeschoolers," AOP Homeschooling, September 5, 2013, http://www.aop.com/blog/why-colleges-are-recruiting-homeschoolers.

47. Camila Domonoske, "Students Have 'Dismaying' Inability to Tell Fake News from Real, Study Finds," NPR, November 23, 2016, http://www.npr.org/sections/thetwo -way/2016/11/23/503129818/study-finds-students-have-dismaying-inability-to-tell-fake -news-from-real.

Chapter 8

1. "The Carnegie Trusts and Institutions," Carnegie Endowment, 2007, http://www .carnegieendowment.org/about/pdfs/carnegie_trusts.pdf.

2. Rafael Heller, "Big Money and Its Influence on K–12 Education: An Interview with Sarah Reckhow," *Phi Delta Kappan*, April 30, 2018, https://kappanonline.org/heller-sarah -reckhow-k12-education-funding-foundations-big-money.

3. William Celis, "Annenberg to Give Education $500 Million over Five Years," *New York Times*, December 17, 1993, http://www.nytimes.com/1993/12/17/us/annenberg-to-give -education-500-million-over-five-years.html.

4. Peter McElroy, "The Annenberg Challenge: Lessons and Legacy," Duke University Sanford School of Public Policy, April 30, 2014, https://cspcs.sanford.duke.edu/sites /default/files/Annenberg%20Challenge%20-%20Peter%20McElroy.pdf; David F. Salisbury, "Private Giving to Public Schools: Does It Work?," Cato Institute, July 19, 2002, http:// www.cato.org/publications/commentary/private-giving-public-schools-does-it-work.

5. Joel L. Fleishman, *The Foundation: A Great American Secret; How Private Wealth Is Changing the World* (New York: PublicAffairs, 2009), 261–83.

6. Carol Innerst, Alexander Russo, and Raymond Domanico, "Can Philanthropy Fix Our Schools? Appraising Walter Annenberg's $500 Million Gift to Public Education," Thomas B. Fordham Foundation, April 2000, https://fordhaminstitute.org/national /research/can-philanthropy-fix-our-schools-appraising-walter-annenbergs-500-million-gift.

7. Heller, "Big Money and Its Influence on K–12 Education."

8. Sarah Reckhow and Jeffrey W. Snyder, "The Expanding Role of Philanthropy in Education Politics," *Educational Researcher* 43, no. 4 (2014): 186–95, https://journals .sagepub.com/doi/abs/10.3102/0013189X14536607.

9. Heller, "Big Money and Its Influence on K–12 Education."

10. Reckhow and Snyder, "The Expanding Role of Philanthropy in Education Politics."

11. Louis Freedberg, "In Strategy Shift, Gates Foundation to Spend Bulk of Education Dollars on 'Locally Driven Solutions,'" EdSource, October 20, 2017, http://www.edsource.org/2017/in-strategy-shift-gates-foundation-to-spend-bulk-of-education-dollars-on-locally-driven-solutions/589145.

12. "Bill Gates' Latest Mission: Fixing America's Schools," Bloomberg, July 17, 2010, http://www.nbcnews.com/id/38282806/ns/business-us_business/t/bill-gates-latest-mission-fixing-americas-schools/#.XBXMHpNKjOQ.

13. Bill Gates, speech to the Council of the Great City Schools, October 19, 2017, https://www.gatesfoundation.org/Media-Center/Speeches/2017/10/Bill-Gates-Council-of-the-Great-City-Schools.

14. Allison Sherry, "Manual's Slow Death," Denver Post, updated May 8, 2016, http://www.denverpost.com/2006/05/05/manuals-slow-death.

15. Sherry, "Manual's Slow Death."

16. Sherry, "Manual's Slow Death."

17. "Gates Funding of Common Core and Related Advocacy," The Federalist, accessed April 20, 2020, https://docs.google.com/spreadsheets/d/16U6R490jgBYvCtxvhdfiEqfcOskqeaCVq6IoqSeFWUY/edit#gid=0.

18. Lyndsey Layton, "How Bill Gates Pulled Off the Swift Common Core Revolution," Washington Post, June 7, 2014, http://www.washingtonpost.com/politics/how-bill-gates-pulled-off-the-swift-common-core-revolution/2014/06/07/a830e32e-ec34-11e3-9f5c-9075d5508f0a_story.html?noredirect=on&utm_term=.ac4821698oc0.

19. Layton, "How Bill Gates Pulled Off the Swift Common Core Revolution."

20. Glenn C. Savage, "Think Tanks, Education and Elite Policy Actors," Australian Educational Researcher, July 22, 2015, 35–53, https://link.springer.com/article/10.1007/s13384-015-0185-0.

21. Layton, "How Bill Gates Pulled Off the Swift Common Core Revolution."

22. Casey Given, "It's Official: The Feds Control Common Core," Jackson Press, March 12, 2014, http://thejacksonpress.org/?p=18690.

23. Bill Gates, "Council of the Great City Schools," Bill and Melinda Gates Foundation, October 19, 2017, https://www.gatesfoundation.org/Media-Center/Speeches/2017/10/Bill-Gates-Council-of-the-Great-City-Schools.

24. Sue Desmond-Hellman, "What If . . . : A Letter from the CEO of the Bill and Melinda Gates Foundation," Bill and Melinda Gates Foundation, 2016, https://www.gatesfoundation.org/2016/ceo-letter.

25. Gates, "Council of the Great City Schools."

26. Gates, "Council of the Great City Schools."

27. Leanna Garfield, "Mark Zuckerberg Once Made a $100 Million Investment in a Major US City to Help Fix Its Schools—Now the Mayor Says the Effort 'Parachuted' in and Failed," Business Insider, May 12, 2018, http://www.businessinsider.com/mark-zuckerberg-schools-education-newark-mayor-ras-baraka-cory-booker-2018-5.

28. Abby Jackson, "Mark Zuckerberg's $100 Million Donation to Newark Public Schools Failed Miserably—Here's Where It Went Wrong," *Business Insider*, September 25, 2015, http://www.businessinsider.com/mark-zuckerbergs-failed-100-million-donation-to -newark-public-schools-2015-9.

29. Stephen Q Cornman and Lei Zhao, "Revenues and Expenditures for Public Elementary and Secondary Education: School Year 2013–14," National Center for Education Statistics, October 2016, http://www.nces.ed.gov/pubs2016/2016301.pdf.

30. Michael Bailin, "Re-Engineering Philanthropy: Field Notes from the Trenches," Georgetown University Waldemar A. Nielsen Issues in Philanthropy Seminar Series, February 21, 2003, http://www.emcf.org/fileadmin/media/PDFs/history/Bailin_Reengineerin Philanthropy.pdf.

31. Fleishman, *The Foundation*.

32. "Success Academy Receives $25 Million Gift from the Robertson Foundation to Expand System of Top-Tier Public Charter Schools," Success Academy, April 12, 2016, http://www.successacademies.org/press-releases/success-academy-receives-25-million -gift-from-the-robertson-foundation-to-expand-system-of-top-tier-public-charter -schools.

33. "Walton Family Foundation Announces Major Investments to Fuel High-Quality School Growth Nationwide," Walton Family Foundation, June 19, 2018, http://www .waltonfamilyfoundation.org/about-us/newsroom/major-investments-to-fuel-high-quality -school-growth-nationwide.

34. "Our Impact," Children's Scholarship Fund, 2018, https://scholarshipfund.org/our -impact.

35. Jenny Anderson, "The Controversial Silicon Valley-Funded Quest to Educate the World's Poorest Kids," *Quartz*, January 22, 2018, http://www.qz.com/1179738/bridge -school.

36. Frank Catalano, "Global Education Technology Investment Hits Record $9.5B, but K-20 Is Only 21% of the Total," GeekWire, January 10, 2018, http://www.geekwire .com/2018/global-education-technology-investment-hits-record-9-5b-k-20-21-total.

37. William A. Schambra, "Think Big vs. Think Small Philanthropy," Hudson Institute, October 31, 2011, https://www.hudson.org/research/8454-think-big-vs-think -small-philanthropy.

38. "Intrinsic Schools," Intrinsic Schools, 2019, http://www.intrinsicschools.org.

39. "CPS Selective Enrollment High Schools: What You Need to Know," ABC7 Chicago, December 14, 2018, http://www.abc7chicago.com/education/cps-selective -enrollment-high-schools-what-you-need-to-know-/4871161.

40. Richard M. Ryan, "Facilitating and Hindering Motivation, Learning, and Well-Being in Schools," in *Handbook of Motivation at School*, ed. Kathryn R. Wentzel and David B. Miele (Abingdon: Routledge, 2016), 96–119.

41. Lauren FitzPatrick, "CPS Moves to Close Two Charter Schools, Denies Applications for Three New Ones," *Chicago Sun-Times*, December 3, 2018, http://www.chicago

.suntimes.com/2018/12/3/18440262/cps-moves-to-close-two-charter-schools-denies
-applications-for-three-new-ones.

42. Sarah Karp, "Chicago Public Schools Withholding Millions from Charter
Schools," WBEZ, April 18, 2019, http://www.wbez.org/shows/wbez-news/chicago-public
-schools-withholding-millions-from-charter-schools-in-spending-standoff/14f9fda0-bd6c
-40a0-8bfb-c2d035dca1f5.

43. "At a Glance," Cristo Rey Network, 2019, http://www.cristoreynetwork.org/about
/at-a-glance.

44. "Innovative Model," Cristo Rey Network, 2019, http://www.cristoreynetwork.org
/schools/innovative-model.

45. "Innovative Model."

46. Getting Smart Staff, "Why Youth Need Social Capital and How Schools Can
Help," *Getting Smart*, September 13, 2018, http://www.gettingsmart.com/2018/09/why
-youth-need-social-capital-and-how-schools-can-help.

47. Katrina Schwartz, "What's So Different about High Tech High Anyway?," KQED,
February 6, 2018, http://www.kqed.org/mindshift/50443/whats-so-different-about-high
-tech-high-anyway.

48. "About Us," High Tech High, 2019, http://www.hightechhigh.org/about-us.

49. "Student Projects," High Tech High, 2018, http://www.hightechhigh.org/student
-work/student-projects.

50. "Breaking Bread," High Tech High, 2018, http://www.hightechhigh.org/hth
/project/breaking-bread.

51. "In Sickness and In Health," High Tech High North County, 2018, http://www
.hightechhigh.org/hthnc/project/in-sickness-and-in-health.

52. "The Bee Project," High Tech Elementary Explorer, 2018, http://www.hightechhigh
.org/htex/project/the-bee-project.

53. "The Challenge," Citizen Schools, 2018, http://www.citizenschools.org/our-model.

54. Jason Bedrick, Jonathan Butcher, and Clint Bolick, "Taking Credit for Education:
How to Fund Education Savings Accounts through Tax Credits," *Cato Institute Policy
Analysis* 785, May 27, 2016, https://papers.ssrn.com/sol3/papers.cfm?abstract_id=2784893.

55. "The Challenge."

56. "Curriculum Library," Citizen Schools, 2018, http://www.citizenschools.org
/curricula?category=STEM.

57. "P-TECH: When Skills Meet Opportunity, Success Happens," IBM, accessed
June 26, 2020, http://www.ibm.com/thought-leadership/ptech/index.html.

58. Kate Hardiman, "IBM's Innovative 6-Year Degree Program Expanding Rapidly,"
Washington Examiner, April 13, 2018, http://www.washingtonexaminer.com/red-alert
-politics/ibms-innovative-6-year-degree-program-expanding-rapidly.

59. "Credentials Matter," Excel in Ed, 2019, http://www.credentialsmatter.org.

60. "School Partner," P-TECH, 2019, http://www.ptech.org/how-it-works/partners
/school-partners.

61. Tara García Mathewson, "Momentum Builds for Career-Focused P-TECH Schools," *Hechinger Report*, August 30, 2018, http://www.hechingerreport.org/momentum -builds-for-career-focused-p-tech-schools.

62. "Khan Lab School," Khan Lab School, 2019, http://www.khanlabschool.org.

63. "Independence Levels." Khan Lab School, September 9, 2017, http://www .khanlabschool.org/independence-levels.

64. "What Makes Us Different?" Khan Lab School, September 28, 2017, http://www .khanlabschool.org/why-khan-lab-school.

65. Chris Weller, "The Founder of Khan Academy Built the Ultimate School for Kids to Work and Play Together—Take a Look Inside," *Business Insider*, October 6, 2017, http://www.businessinsider.com/khan-lab-school-tour-inside-sal-khans-newest-school -2017-10.

Chapter 9

1. 268 U.S. 510, 535 (1925).

2. Home School Legal Defense Association, "History of HSLDA," Sept. 19, 2019, https://hslda.org/post/history-of-hslda.

3. 347 U.S. 483, 493 (1954).

4. See, e.g., Tanner Colby, "How the Left's Embrace of Busing Hurt the Cause of Integration," *Slate*, Feb. 3, 2014, https://slate.com/human-interest/2014/02/how-the-lefts -embrace-of-busing-hurt-the-cause-of-integration.html.

5. 411 U.S. 1 (1973).

6. Natalie Wexler, "Why a 'Constitutional Right to Education' Won't Mean Much," *Forbes*, April 27, 2020, https://www.forbes.com/sites/nataliewexler/2020/04/27/why-a -constitutional-right-to-education-wont-mean-much/#218bdd7075b9.

7. Adam Clark and Disha Raychaudhuri, "Here's What Every N.J. District Spends Per Student," NJ.com, Aug. 20, 2019, https://www.nj.com/education/2019/08/heres-what -every-nj-district-spends-per-student.html.

8. See generally Jared S. Buzsin, "Beyond School Finance: Refocusing Education Reform Litigation to Realize the Deferred Dream of Education Equality and Adequacy," *Emory Law Journal* 62, no. 6 (2013), http://law.emory.edu/elj/content/volume-62/issue-6 /comments/beyond-school-finance.html.

9. Horne v. Flores, 557 U.S. 443, 467 (2009).

10. See Buzsin, "Beyond School Finance"; "Education Policy Litigation as Devolu-tion," *Harvard Law Review* 128 (2015), https://harvardlawreview.org/2015/01/education -policy-litigation-as-devolution.

11. Quoted in Dmitri Mehlhorn, "Commentary: Vergara's Dissenting Justices Write for History," LA School Report, Aug. 24, 2016, http://laschoolreport.com/commentary -vergaras-dissenting-justices-write-for-history.

12. 413 U.S. 756, 782 n. 38.

13. See Clint Bolick, *Voucher Wars* (Washington, DC: Cato Institute, 2003).

14. 536 U.S. 639, 653 (2002).

15. *Id.* at 658 (Breyer, J., dissenting).

16. Quoted in Clint Bolick, *David's Hammer: The Case for an Activist Judiciary* (Washington, DC: Cato Institute, 2007), 138.

17. Owens v. Colorado Congress of Parents, 92 P.3d 933 (Colo. 2004); Bush v. Holmes, 919 So.2d 392 (Fla. 2006).

18. "Nevada: Education Savings Accounts."

19. Espinoza v. Montana Department of Revenue, No. 18-1195, slip op. (U.S. June 30, 2020) at 2–5 (Alito, J., concurring).

20. *Id.* at 10 (Opinion of the Court).

21. *Id.* at 13.

22. *Id.* at 20.

Chapter 10

1. Marc Andreessen, "It's Time to Build," Andreessen Horowitz (blog), April 18, 2020, https://a16z.com/2020/04/18/its-time-to-build.

2. Patrick R. Gibbons, "The Gilberts Ride the Whirlwind," *RedefinED*, August 8, 2019, http://www.redefinedonline.org/2019/08/the-gilberts-ride-the-whirlwind.

3. Gibbons, "The Gilberts Ride the Whirlwind."

4. Jeb Bush, "Florida's Intuitive Letter Grades Produce Results," *Education Next*, November 28, 2016, http://www.educationnext.org/floridas-intuitive-letter-grades -produce-results-forum-jeb-bush-accountability.

5. Cara Fitzpatrick, Lisa Gartner, and Michael LaForgia, "Failure Factories," *Tampa Bay Times*, August 14, 2015, http://www.tampabay.com/projects/2015/investigations /pinellas-failure-factories/5-schools-segregation.

6. Fitzpatrick, Gartner, and LaForgia, "Failure Factories."

7. Fitzpatrick, Gartner, and LaForgia, "Failure Factories."

8. Cecelia Elena Rouse et al., "Feeling the Florida Heat? How Low-Performing Schools Respond to Voucher and Accountability Pressure," *American Economic Journal: Economic Policy* 5, no. 2 (May 2013): 251–81, http://www.jstor.org/stable/43189334.

9. "Advanced Placement: State Provides Financial Incentives for AP Courses," Education Commission of the States, May 15, 2020, http://ecs.force.com/mbdata/MBQuest SNR?Rcp=AP02.

10. John Kennedy, "GOP Pushes Pay Raises for Teachers, State Workers in Florida: Genuine or Election Year Politics?" *USA Today*, February 10, 2020, https://www.usatoday .com/story/news/education/2020/02/09/florida-teachers-state-workers-republicans-push -pay-raises/4707553002.

11. Patrick R. Gibbons, "Options on the Rise: 1.7 Million Florida Students Exercise School Choice," *RedefinED*, February 2, 2018, http://www.redefinedonline.org/2018/01 /changing-landscapes-2016-17-school-choice.

12. "Florida's Charter Schools," Office of Independent Education and Parental Choice, Florida Department of Education, September 2018, http://www.fldoe.org/core/fileparse .php/7696/urlt/Charter-Sept-2018.pdf.

13. Kristen M Clark and Kyra Gurney, "Governor Signs Controversial Schools Bill into Law," *Miami Herald*, June 15, 2017, http://www.miamiherald.com/news/local /education/article156299239.html.

14. "In Case You Missed It: Governor Ron DeSantis Commends Florida Legislature for Passage of School Choice Expansion and Key Education Priorities," Office of Governor Ron DeSantis, May 6, 2019, https://www.flgov.com/2019/05/06/in-case-you -missed-it-governor-ron-desantis-commends-florida-legislature-for-passage-of-school -choice-expansion-and-key-education-priorities.

15. "Schools of Hope," Florida Department of Education, 2017, http://www.fldoe.org /schools/school-choice/other-school-choice-options/schools-of-hope.

16. "Schools of Hope."

17. "In Case You Missed It."

18. "Basic Program Facts," Step Up for Students, 2017, http://www.stepupforstudents .org/newsroom/basic-program-facts.

19. "Basic Program Facts."

20. "Florida Tax Credit Scholarship Program," ExcelinEd, 2018, http://www.excelined .org/wp-content/uploads/2018/08/Opportunity.TCS_.FLTCSOverview-1.pdf.

21. Jason Bedrick, Lindsey Burke, and Robert C. Enlow, "Four Reasons for Preserving the Autonomy of SGOs," Cato Institute, December 4, 2015, https://www.cato.org /publications/commentary/four-reasons-preserving-autonomy-sgos.

22. Leslie Postal, "Nation's Report Card: 'Something Very Good Is Happening in Florida,'" *Orlando Sentinel*, May 3, 2018, http://www.orlandosentinel.com/features/ education/school-zone/os-os-florida-naep-test-scores-20180409-story.html.

23. "The Nation's Report Card: Florida Overview," National Association for Educational Progress, 2019, https://www.nationsreportcard.gov/profiles/stateprofile /overview/FL?cti=PgTab_OT&chort=1&sub=MAT&sj=FL&fs=Grade&st=MN&year =2013R3&sg=Genderpercent3A+Male+vs.+Female&sgv=Difference&ts=Single+Year&tss =2013R3-2013R3&sfj=NP.

24. Kyra Gurney, "Charter Students, Especially Minorities, Score Better on Florida Tests, Report Finds," *Miami Herald* , May 8, 2017, http://www.miamiherald.com/news /local/education/article148915414.html.

25. Jason Bedrick and Lindsey M. Burke, "Surveying Florida Scholarship Families," EdChoice, 2018, http://www.edchoice.org/research/surveying-florida-scholarship-families.

26. "Newpoint Charter Schools Owner Marcus May Gets 20 Years in Prison, Fined $5 Million," *Pensacola News Journal*, November 13, 2018, http://www.pnj.com/story/news /crime/2018/11/13/newpoint-charter-schools-owner-sentenced-prison-fined-5-million /1992647002/.

27. "Florida's Charter Schools."

28. Lloyd Dunkelberger, "Report Shows Florida Latinos Bridging Education Gap," *Florida Politics*, June 15, 2018, http://www.floridapolitics.com/archives/266408-report -shows-florida-latinos-bridging-education-gap.

29. Matthew Chingos and Daniel Kuehn, "The Effects of Statewide Private School Choice on College Enrollment and Graduation," Urban Institute, September 27, 2017, https://www.urban.org/research/publication/effects-statewide-private-school-choice -college-enrollment-and-graduation.

30. Matthew Chingos and David Kuehn, "The Effects of Statewide Private School Choice on College Enrollment and Graduation: An Update," Urban Institute, February 2019, https://www.urban.org/sites/default/files/publication/99728/the_effects_of_the _florida_tax_credit_scholarship_program_on_college_enrollment_and_graduation_2.pdf.

31. Chingos and Kuehn, "The Effects of Statewide Private School Choice on College Enrollment and Graduation."

32. William Mattox, "Opinion: 'School Choice Moms' Tipped the Governor's Florida Race," *Wall Street Journal*, November 20, 2018, http://www.wsj.com/articles/school-choice -moms-tipped-the-governors-florida-race-1542757880.

33. John Rosales, "Five Reasons Why Florida's Andrew Gillum Is Public Education's Pick for Governor," National Education Association: Education Votes, October 15, 2018, http://www.educationvotes.nea.org/2018/09/14/five-reasons-why-floridas-andrew-gillum -is-public-educations-pick-for-governor.

34. Many European countries, notably Finland and Switzerland, offer students a number of professional apprenticeship positions through which they can obtain real-world skills as well as preview a variety of jobs.

35. Frederick Hess, "EdChoice Academy," presentation at EdChoice Academy, October 15, 2019.

36. Harper Lee, *To Kill a Mockingbird* (New York: Grand Central Publishing, 1988), 36.

37. Corey A. DeAngelis, "The Highly Positive Impacts of Vouchers," Cato Institute, March 28, 2018, http://www.cato.org/blog/highly-positive-impacts-vouchers.

38. Robert C. Enlow, "The K–12 Financial Cliff: What States Could Face If Students Switch Schooling Sectors," EdChoice, April 20, 2020, https://www.edchoice.org/engage /the-k-12-financial-cliff-what-states-could-face-if-students-switch-schooling-sectors.

About the Authors

Clint Bolick is a justice on the Arizona Supreme Court and a research fellow with the Hoover Institution. As cofounder of the Institute for Justice, Bolick defended school choice programs against legal challenges across the nation, culminating in the milestone US Supreme Court victory in *Zelman v. Simmons-Harris*. A prolific author, Bolick has written, most recently, *Immigration Wars: Forging an American Solution* (coauthored with Jeb Bush) and *David's Hammer: The Case for an Activist Judiciary*. Bolick teaches constitutional law as an adjunct professor at the Arizona State University and University of Arizona schools of law. Throughout his career, he has championed educational opportunities, especially for children who lack them. He is a husband, father of four, and grandfather of two.

Kate J. Hardiman works as a legal fellow at a law firm in Washington, DC, and is concurrently obtaining her JD from Georgetown Law School. Previously, Hardiman taught at a Catholic high school in Chicago through Notre Dame's Alliance for Catholic Education MEd program. She is a regular contributor to the *Washington Examiner* opinion page on education issues and has been published in *The Hill, RealClearBooks, Education Post, The College Fix*, and *Minding the Campus*. She is a 2019 Claremont Institute Publius Fellow and a 2020 Alliance Defending Freedom Blackstone Fellow. Hardiman believes that school choice policies improve the lives of children and strengthen our nation. She plans to pursue a career in education law and policy.

Index